P9-DWW-718

My PARIS MARKET COOKBOOK

My PARIS MARKET COOKBOOK

A CULINARY TOUR OF FRENCH FLAVORS AND SEASONAL RECIPES

EMILY DILLING

PHOTOS BY NICHOLAS BALL

Skyhorse Publishing

Skyhorse Publishing books may be purchased in bulk at special discounts for sales promotion, corporate gifts, fund-raising, or educational purposes. Special editions can also be created to specifications. For details, contact the Special Sales Department, Skyhorse Publishing, 307 West 36th Street, 11th Floor, New York, NY 10018 or info@ skyhorsepublishing.com.

Skyhorse® and Skyhorse Publishing® are registered trademarks of Skyhorse Publishing, Inc.®, a Delaware corporation.

Visit our website at www.skyhorsepublishing.com.

10 9 8 7 6 5 4 3 2 1

Library of Congress Cataloging-in-Publication Data is available on file.

Jacket design by Laura Klynstra
Front cover photographs: Shutterstock
Back cover photographs by Nicholas Ball
Author photograph by Anna Brones

Print ISBN: 978-1-63450-584-0
Ebook ISBN: 978-1-63450-864-3

Printed in China

To my parents, two amazing independent producers,
and to my Paris ladies, my favorite local treasures.

"Cookbooks will give you ideas . . . but the market will give you dinner."

—Judy Rodgers

CONTENTS

INTRODUCTION

The *Paris Paysanne* blog, which inspired this book, began in the summer of 2010. I had just returned to Paris from a trip to the United States where I toured the West Coast, visiting friends from San Francisco to Seattle. My travels brought me in contact with food activists and engaged eaters, from Slow Food–inspired chefs to farmers' market fanatics to excited foodies who would talk to me of cow shares and edible forests. When I got back to Paris, which I had called home for five years at that point, I was excited to join the French equivalent of the growing food movement I had seen in the United States. It didn't take long for me to realize that my two homes were worlds apart when it came to food activism. France, whose cuisine is based on a rich culinary tradition which has provided the grammar for gastronomy, seemed to be suffering from the adverse effects of resting on one's laurels. While the capital city has always had a noteworthy food scene including some of the best, most highly rated restaurants in the world, good food in your average restaurant appeared harder and harder to find. Quality meals had seemingly all but disappeared from the corner *bistrot*, where frozen and vacuum-packed foods are habitually reheated and served. The locally grown seasonal produce that had so excited me at farmers' markets in the States was a rare find at Paris *marchés*, where farmers were becoming less and less present, replaced with resellers hawking wholesale, industrial produce from as far as South America. Among all the disappointments in the Paris food scene, the absence of farmers and locally grown produce at the market shocked and saddened me the most. These very markets were an inspiration to great chefs and food icons such as Julia Child and Alice Waters, and now they remained a shadow of their former selves and a false representation of greater days.

So I began visiting the markets in search of independent producers, which I added to my growing "Farmers at Paris Markets" map with each new discovery. Market visits led to more encounters and questions, as I started talking to the chefs, coffee roasters, and craft brewers that made up the "eat local" movement in Paris. I began exploring the art and savoir faire behind making some of the country's most amazing natural wines, and learned about the *terre* behind France's *terroir*. I've met amazing, passionate people along the way and have never ceased to be amazed by the creativity, dedication, and integrity of these artisans.

It seems fitting that the idea for the blog, and later this book, all started at the markets. For me, even the simplest neighborhood marché is a crossroads of culture, community, and customs. Whenever I visit a new city, the first thing I do is find the local market. I can think of no better way to expose oneself to a new place and its people than by going to a market. Markets bring neighbors together. They introduce us to the people who grow our food, the people who feed us. They are a source of new ideas, inspiration, and recipes. They are the way we participate in the most basic and fundamental ritual shared by all humans—shopping for the ingredients that we will take home, make into a meal, and share with the people we love.

I hope that *My Paris Market Cookbook* brings you a little bit of the magic of Paris markets, the joy of locally grown food, and an appreciation of the people who bring us nourishment and happiness—whether it be a recipe, an immersion into a busy Saturday morning at the marché, or a place to get the perfect filtered coffee while in town. Most of all, I hope this guide will bring you a step closer to supporting the people in your life, no matter where you are, that put food on your table.

A FEW NOTES ON THE RECIPES IN
MY PARIS MARKET COOKBOOK

All the recipes in this book are inspired by people and places that I've come to love while living in Paris and exploring France. I have tried to choose simple recipes that are representative of classic French cuisine and that concentrate on quality, locally sourced ingredients. The selection of seasonal recipes that you'll find in *My Paris Market Cookbook* were intentionally chosen because they require only a few ingredients, which can, for the most part, be easily found at your local farmers' market.

It is my hope that the recipes included in this book will not only be enjoyable once prepared, but also fun to serve to family and friends. If you've never made a cheese soufflé or madeleines, I hope that you decide that this is the time to try. By exploring the recipes in this book, and the stories of the city that inspired them, I hope you will find that French cooking, like life, is actually not that complicated—you just need good ingredients!

FINDING FARMERS AT PARIS MARKETS

This book is intended to be a guide and resource for anyone who wants to eat well in Paris. Whether you are visiting from afar or have lived in Paris all your life, *My Paris Market Cookbook* offers insight into the best cafés, restaurants, bars, shops, and market stands for locally grown seasonal produce and products that reflect the essence of French terroir.

HOW DO YOU FIND A FARMER?

Spotting a farmer at a Paris market is not always an easy task, especially to the untrained eye or non-francophone. Unlike farmers' markets in the United States, French farmers don't necessarily advertise the name or location of their farm at their market stand. There is also no universal system indicating whether or not the vendor is the actual grower of the produce or merely a reseller. However, there are a few key words and telltale signs that you have found a real farmer at your market. Here are a few that I live by:

Producteur: In French, *producteur* means "producer," but it also indicates that the person in question is an independent grower, usually on a small family farm. If you see this written anywhere on a stand's signage it is safe to assume that all, or most of, the products you will find there were grown by the person that is

Farm fresh produce at Marché Biologique des Batignolles.

Locally sourced vegetables at Marché d'Aligre.

selling them to you. You may also see signs saying that the fruits and vegetables are *de notre production*, or grown by the vendor him or herself.

Maraîcher: Similarly to *producteur*, *maraîcher* indicates that the fruits and vegetables (or at least a selection of them) are homegrown. *Maraîcher* can be translated as "market gardener," or farmer. Usually these producers only grow vegetables on their farm and have no livestock or other food production on site.

Île-de-France: This refers to Paris and its surrounding region, made up of eight different *départements*: Paris, Essonne, Hauts-de-Seine, Seine Saint Denis, Seine-et-Marne, Val-de-Marne, Val-d'Oise, and Yvelines. Informally referred to as *la région parisienne*, produce grown here is about as local as a shopper in Paris can get.

Dirty seasonal produce: Skip the stands stocked with winter strawberries and stop once you've spotted worn-out wooden crates filled with earth-covered seasonal produce. Usually these stands will have less of a selection, but all the produce will be representative of what the farmer is actually growing and what is truly in season.

Long lines: A testament to the power of quality produce, it always makes me happy to see that a farmer's stand invariably has the longest lines. Even without being overtly advertised as such, independent farmers find a loyal following at the city's markets. Led by what seems to be an innate appreciation for homegrown, nourishing food, shoppers are willing to wait a little bit longer and have a little less choice in exchange for high quality fruits and vegetables.

Farmer Marc Mascetti at Marché Monge.

AUTUMN

Autumn is a season for strolling in Paris. Luxembourg Garden fills with freshly fallen leaves that crinkle satisfactorily underfoot, and walks along the Seine are accompanied by a crisp blue sky reflected in the river's water. The shades of this time of year are reflected in the kaleidoscope of colors at the market. Orange and green gourds seduce shoppers as they peruse purple cauliflower and yellow carrots. Red apples and speckled green pears catch the eye at early morning market stands, reminding us that a new season has arrived.

This season also brings the grape harvests, or *vendanges*, which are commemorated by Montmartre's Fête des Vendanges in early October and the celebration of the arrival of Beaujolais Nouveau in November. Markets, restaurants, and wine bars embrace the spirit of the season by proposing products that embody the essence of autumn, with its earthy vegetables, open bottles of young red wine, and a warm welcome to the cold days to come.

In Season: *apples, beets, brussels sprouts, celery root, carrots, figs, parsnips, potatoes, radishes, Swiss chard, turnips, walnuts, wild mushrooms*

MARCHÉ PRÉSIDENT WILSON

AVENUE DU PRÉSIDENT WILSON, 75016
M° IÉNA (LINE 9)
OPEN: WEDNESDAY AND SATURDAY, 7:00 A.M.–3:00 P.M.

Marché Président Wilson welcomes visitors with overflowing flower stands at both ends and friendly vendors in between. At Marché President Wilson, there is a large selection of artisanal meat and cheese stands in addition to a natural/organic wine vendor. The tree-lined streets turn golden during this enchanting season and the produce embraces the ocher shades of summer transitioning to fall. The market is home to two local producers as well as an organic vendor, C'Bio, which sources produce from the Rungis market in addition to working closely with an independent farmer in the Île-de-France region. American by birth but French by choice, the friendly Suzanne advises visitors to the C'Bio stand on how to prepare the exciting fruit and vegetable varieties on offer. You can also buy C'Bio produce at Marché Auguste Blanqui in the 13th arrondissement (137 boulevard Auguste Blanqui).

Autumn has a special appeal to admirers of eccentric vegetables. The magic of this fleeting period of transition between the seasons is not lost on famed farmer Joël Thiébault, who relishes the overlap of fall and summer, a time when the best of both seasons converge at his market stand.

The Thiébault family has been selling vegetables in Paris markets since 1873 and Joël continues his family's work through his constant quest for *légumes oubliés*—heirloom vegetables—which he cultivates on his farm in Carrières-sur-Seine, just twelve miles from Paris. Joël is also present at Marché Gros-la-Fontaine, also in the 16th arrondissement (37 rue Gros), on Tuesday and Friday.

Ask Joël what his favorite vegetables are and he'll respond with a playful smile, "The ones I haven't grown yet." The truth is that Thiébault loves all his vegetables equally, with a devotion that is clear in his encyclopedic knowledge of every variety he sells.

Early morning visits to Joël's stand at the market offer insight into what the choosiest chefs in Paris restaurants will be serving on their *carte du jour*. Restaurateurs and other guests of honor gather in what resembles a VIP lounge behind the vegetable stand, where dignitaries of the cuisine scene are inspired by the exceptional produce that surrounds them.

KRISTEN BEDDARD: A LA RECHERCHE DU CHOU PERDU

When Kristen Beddard moved to Paris in 2011 she had a number of challenges to contend with, including leaving behind her career to move with her husband to a foreign city, saying goodbye to her beloved New York, and settling into a new life in a country whose language she didn't speak. Of all the evident obstacles that she had to face, it was the unexpected surprise of the city's lack of kale that Kristen decided to tackle head-on. An avid kale consumer since childhood, the absence of this particular leafy green at Paris shops and markets was unsettling to Kristen, who responded by launching *The Kale Project.* Kristen began spreading the word about the popular cabbage variety on her website while reaching out to local farmers to encourage them to cultivate locally grown kale for Parisians and beyond. Three years later, *le chou kale* has become a more and more common sight at markets and organic shops in Paris. Since helping to usher in a new era of kale in her adopted home, Kristen has now started to concentrate on other légumes oubliés and generally underrated vegetables. Author of the book *Savez-vous manger les choux?*, Kristen is now bringing her love of the brassica family and locally grown vegetables to the French in a city and a language that she has learned to make her own!

MARCHÉ CONVENTION

RUE CONVENTION, 75015
M° CONVENTION (LINE 12)
OPEN: TUESDAY, THURSDAY, AND SUNDAY, 7:00 A.M.–2:30 P.M.

Exploring the 15th arrondissement of Paris almost feels like traveling in time. This traditional, and largely residential, part of Paris is full of classic cafés and corner bistrots. This conservative quarter has not been affected by foreign influence or trendy establishments, and butchers and bakers proudly display traditional French products in their shop windows.

Marché Convention lines rue Convention ending at place Charles Vallin, where you will find the Maison Lenoble stand. Located in the Île-de-France, this local farm's stand is a great spot to stop as summer transitions to autumn. Late summer eggplant and bell peppers mingle with cabbage, lettuce, and leaks. Rarer vegetable varieties, such as watermelon radish and heirloom tomatoes, can also be found here. If you're not planning on visiting in the 15th arrondissement, you can also find the Lenoble family's stand at Marché Berthier (boulevard de Reims, 17th arrondissement) and Marché Point du Jour (avenue de Versailles, 16th arrondissement).

PARIS FOOD TRENDS

The overwhelming influence of American food trends in Paris has reached a fever pitch in recent years, marked by an obsession with tacos and cupcakes and other United States favorites. Maybe the most surprising American import was the arrival of the food truck trend. In the blink of an eye, food trucks had taken over the city and were finding a way to fit into a culture that adores its sit-down lunches and one-hour midday breaks.

California native Kristin Frederick is credited with spearheading the food truck movement in Paris when she got behind the wheel of Le Camion Qui Fume in 2012. Her burger truck embraced quality ingredients and some of the best *frites* in the city, making it a hit with Parisians and inspiring a fleet of food trucks to follow. Some variations on the mobile food concept have missed the mark (a ten-euro grilled cheese sandwich is a tough sell in any city) but many food trucks have adapted the idea to reflect local specialties. The Bugelski deli food truck has taken up the challenge of locally sourcing its ingredients, featuring *le vrai Jambon de Paris* (page 40) and many vegetables that are grown in the region. Increasingly more engaged in the *manger local* movement, the Île-de-France even has its own food truck, which proudly sports the innovative "Des produits d'ici, cuisinés ici" label (page 81). The concept of standing in line and finding a nearby spot to stop and eat (especially in a city whose parks usually keep their grassy areas off-limits for picnics) makes the food truck trend a bit perplexing to the French, but demonstrating that you can prepare locally sourced ingredients to make simple, good food in a small space is proving to Parisians that even the most modest spaces can be used to produce quality cuisine.

Another novel business model sprung from is the result of the recent emergence of cafés that use locally roasted beans (page 83). These coffee shops have quickly spread across the city in the past few years. Restricted in space and what meals can be prepared on site, but also committed to excellence in both food and coffee, many of these innovative cafés have decided to outsource some of the work, bringing in specialty chefs and bakers to prepare the breakfast and lunch options they serve in-house. Each café seeks to differentiate itself and offer exciting and unexpected foods. This is a tall order in a city that loves its croissants and *pain au chocolat*, but also offers the opportunity to be both creative and a taste trendsetter. Emperor Norton, one of the city's favorite food curators and caterers, was one of the first teams to take up the challenge raised by these craft cafés. The talented pair behind Emperor Norton is married couple Omid Tavallai and Alannah McPherson Tavallai, West Coast natives who made their way to Paris for Omid's job. In order to pass the time and enjoy the comfort foods they missed from home, Omid and Alannah experimented in their kitchen, posting photos of the finished meals on a blog as they went. Omid and Alannah quickly noticed that the biggest fans of their American-inspired cooking were ex-pats in Paris. And so was born Emperor Norton, a specialty catering enterprise that quickly began delivering everything from pickles and hot dogs to trendy bars

and donuts and fresh granola to coffee shops around the city. While the team still provides savory selections for a few Paris addresses (pickles and hot dogs can be found at Glass, 7 rue Frochot 9th arrondissement) the focus has fallen mostly on sweets, including comforting classics such as banana bread, *Snickerdoodles* (page 54), and cakes. Regular spots to enjoy their freshly baked goods include Téléscope (5 rue Villedo, 1st arrondissement), Fondation (16 rue Dupetit Thours, 3rd arrondissement), Boot Café (19 rue du Pont aux Choux, 3rd arrondissement), and Loustic (40 rue Chapon, 3rd arrondissement).

MARCHÉ DES ENFANTS ROUGES

39 RUE DE BRETAGNE, 75003
Mᵒ FILLES DE CALVAIRE (LINE 8)
OPEN: TUESDAY–SATURDAY, 8:30 A.M.–7:30 P.M., SUNDAY, 8:30 A.M.–2:00 P.M.

Created as an orphanage for young pensioners clad in red, the Marché des Enfants Rouges was transformed into a market in 1615 and has remained as such throughout various renovations, most recently in 2000 when the market had its latest makeover. A favorite lunchtime spot among tourists and locals alike, the latest incarnation of the market is equipped with long lunch counters and scattered picnic tables that fill up during the lunch rush.

World cuisine is abundantly represented, with market specialties that include fresh pasta from the Italian deli counter, a Moroccan stand serving a lamb tagine of certain renown, and Japanese bento boxes.

Produce, fish, meat, flowers, and cheese stands are open and on sale during regular market hours (7:00 a.m.–2:00 p.m.), and the market even has

one Île-de-France farmer, with a small stand in the back right-hand corner of the market.

The draw of this market remains the hot lunch options from around the globe. A favorite stand is kept by the animated Alain, who sells his fresh baked breads and prepares crêpes for hungry visitors on site. The true culinary treasure at Alain's stand is a specialty from southern France called *Socca* (page 26). Though not as foreign as the neighboring Japanese or African fare, these chickpea pancakes are surprisingly difficult to find in Paris and attract fans from near and far.

Using a simple chickpea flour-based batter, Alain makes up for his lack of a traditional wood-burning stove by flipping socca pancakes on his multi-purpose hot plates, producing an impressive likeness to what one would find in Nice, the capital city of socca.

LES VENDANGES:
THE WINE COUNTRY'S HARVEST SEASON

The French don't have a tradition of going away to summer camps in their youth, but the yearly vendanges, or grape harvests, are probably the closest the French get to the sleepaway camp experience. Harvesters made up of students and adults in need of a getaway flock to wine growing regions and spend their end-of-summer days picking grapes and enjoying the outdoors, with newfound friends and a renewed appreciation of the beauty of the French countryside.

The harvest season is a time of both excruciating physical labor and extreme conviviality. Winemakers assemble teams of harvesters that spend their days in the grapevines, going row by row, picking and sorting good grapes from the bad, vigilantly keeping an eye out for rot and mildew that could contaminate the wine. This is a crucial moment in the winemaking process and there is pressure to pick grapes at the right time, to be sure that the bunches that will later be pressed and put in a barrel are of the highest quality. The harvest can be a stressful time for the winemaker, and back-breaking for the harvesters, but that doesn't stop anyone from enjoying this unique experience in the vines and with each other.

The ambience at each vineyard during the vendanges varies. Small natural winemakers provide the most intimate experience, often inviting interested harvesters to participate not only in the picking of the grapes but in other aspects of the winemaking process as well. Communal lunches, strolls among the grapes, and encounters with new people and local winemakers are often added benefits of taking part in the harvest. The arrival of so many people from around the country, and sometimes the world, who come to work in the vines brings a new energy to the region, creating a festive and familial atmosphere.

In September 2014, I decided to participate in the grape harvest for the first time. Making what was, I would later find out, one of the best decisions of my life, I reached out to natural winemaker Noëlla Morantin and asked if I could join her team of *vendangeurs*. I met Noëlla a few times at wine tastings and developed a bit of a canine crush on Panache, the official winery dog, at that year's La Dive Bouteille tasting in Saumur. Other than these brief meetings, Noëlla barely knew me, so I was pleasantly surprised when she agreed to have me join her team for that year's harvest.

Noëlla and fellow winemaker Laurent Saillard cultivate 12 hectares (30 acres) of grapevines in the Loir-et-Cher region of the Loire Valley. Together they tend to every aspect of the winemaking process, from farming and harvesting to barreling and bottling. They manage every step of the process with attention and respect for the principles of biodynamic and natural winemaking. It is a huge job that they mostly do alone, with the extra helping hands of the harvest season and seasonal employees when needed.

The aches and pains of bending and kneeling to pick grape bunch after grape bunch are the price you pay to be a part of the humbling experience of doing the work that will result in that year's vintage. The harvest involves picking grapes, of course, but it's so much more than that. While at Noëlla and Laurent's vineyard I was able to share in the fascinating and slightly magical process of making natural wine, from hand-picking grapes, removing them from their stems using artisanal methods, to crushing still-warm-from-the-sun Gamay grapes with my bare feet.

During my time in the Loire, I met a group of passionate and extraordinary people. We cooked together, stargazed together, went to bed soaked in moonlight and woke up with the sun together. For visitors unaccustomed to life in the vines, the harvest season is a moment in time dedicated to finding harmony with nature and taking time to slow down and enjoy the beauty of your surroundings.

Exploring the enchanting Loire Valley also brought me to the doorsteps of talented winemakers such as Thierry Puzelat, René and Agnès Mosse, Hervé Villemade, Christophe Foucher, and Christian Venier. Visiting the various vineyards and meeting the people behind my favorite wines reminded me of why I was inspired to move to France in the first place: to immerse myself in a culture that takes pride in the process of making products well and with integrity, and to spend time with people who appreciate the results of these efforts.

I never went to summer camp as a kid. But if I missed out on something by not going to camp, I more than made up for it during the vendanges in the Loire, where I rediscovered a love of nature, learned what goes into the wine that I love, and met people who I will hold dear to my heart forever.

MARCHÉ BASTILLE

BOULEVARD RICHARD LENOIR, 75011
M° RICHARD LENOIR (LINE 5)
OPEN: THURSDAY AND SUNDAY, 7:00 A.M.–2:30 P.M.

Along the tree-lined boulevard Richard Lenoir in the 11th arrondissement, autumn leaves turn a rusty red and fall and tumble amidst the bustling stands of the Marché Bastille. Starting near the famous monument to the fallen prison and continuing along the boulevard on an island spotted with parks, fountains, and benches, the market attracts both locals with stalks of leeks poking out of bags and backpacks and tourists with their cameras at the ready. The friendly rapport between vendors and shoppers makes one

Shopping at M. and Mme. Baudry's stand at Marché Bastille.

feel instantly at home in this charming and chatty market that is home to a handful of local farmers.

M. Baudry, a farmer from the Eure region in Normandy, sells heirloom varieties, including black and purple radishes and bright yellow and purple cauliflower. You will also find game fowl such as duck, pheasant, and quail at his stand. Autumn months bring heirloom varieties of carrots, cauliflower, cabbage, and rutabaga.

Les Vergers de Picardie sells fruits from their orchard at this and many other Paris markets. Apples and pears are on offer, as well as freshly pressed juice and a selection of other from-the-farm products that vary depending on the season. In autumn these growers will bring endives and walnuts from neighboring farms to complement their own selection of seasonal fruits.

Arnaud, a former *patissier* (baker) and vendor at Les Vergers de Picardie will gladly instruct curious shoppers on how to make a traditional French *Tarte aux Pommes* (page 52). The Picardie native points out that there are

varying regional recipes in different parts of France. In Brittany, milk and crème fraîche are added to apple tartes (and to almost everything in that region!). In Picardie, compote or apple sauce is used as a first layer before sweet baking apples are added to the pie.

EAT LOCALLY, DRINK NATURALLY: DISCOVERING *VIN NATURE*

While the "eat local" movement seems considerably more developed in most parts of the United States, the excitement around natural wine and a "less is more" approach to winemaking is booming in France. *Natural wine* is an umbrella term that has been highly contested by both proponents and naysayers of the movement. As a result, these low-intervention wines go by many names in France (and abroad) including *vin naturel*, *vin nature*, *vin vivant*, or even *jus de raisin fermenté* (fermented grape juice). For true adherents to the "nothing added, nothing taken away" approach to winemaking the key to making an honest wine (by whatever name you choose to call it) is making sure that every part of the winemaking process—from farming to bottling—embraces a biodynamic and sustainable approach to winemaking that respects the local terroir and rejects additives or synthetic manipulation of the grapes.

Natural wines often break the mold because their winemakers are not concerned with, or interested in, replicating the tastes or nuances of previous years' bottles from the same vineyard or region. Natural winemakers let each vintage express the story of that year, with its fluctuations in weather, changes in seasons, and other environmental influences becoming part of the narrative inside each bottle. The refusal to add chemical stabilizers or flavors, such as sulfites and preservatives, results in a wine that is a true expression of a place and time.

Natural wines have found a warm welcome in Paris. Selections from small vineyards and engaged winemakers are more and more common in the city's restaurants, wine bars, and wine shops. A growing number of *cavistes*, or wine merchants, are now dedicating themselves working exclusively with vin nature and the small-scale winemakers that produce it.

Early proponents of natural wine include the dedicated and knowledgeable cavistes at La Cave des Papilles (35 rue Daguerre, 14th arrondissement),

Natural wine at Crus et Découvertes.

which is practically a library of the history of natural wine, stocking hard-to-find bottles and older vintages of favorites winemakers in the world of vin nature. Crus et Découvertes (7 rue Paul Bert, 11th arrondissement) is a small and selective boutique where you can find carefully chosen bottles and a thoughtful, passionate staff. Neighborhood institution Le Verre Volé sells bottles from their original restaurant location (67 rue de Lancry, 10th arrondissement) and have also expanded to include an *épicerie* (page 137) as well as a cave (38 rue Oberkampf, 11th arrondissement). The man who literally wrote the book on *Vin Vivant*, Pierre Jancou, inspired a small but exciting selection of bottles you can take away or enjoy on-site at the wine bar he founded, Vivant Cave (43 rue des Petite Écuries, 10th arrondissement), which is located next to the chef's famed restaurant.

Le Vin en Tête has two boutiques in Paris (48 rue Notre Dame de Lorette, 9th arrondissement and 30 rue des Batignolles, 17th arrondissement) as well

Lunchtime at Le Siffleur des Ballons.

as L'Etabli, a wine bar located in the 17th arrondissement. Dedicated to not only selling natural wines, but also educating consumers, the stores organize regular tastings (page 135) where customers can meet invited winemakers and discover wines from regions all around France.

A more recent addition to the natural wine scene is Le Siffleur des Ballons (34 rue de Cîteaux, 12th arrondissement), where the charming Thomas and Tristan have kept the wine flowing and the cheese plates full since the shop opened on November 15th (Beaujolais Nouveau day) in 2012. The store is open in the mornings and afternoons and the varied selection of French natural wines leaves much room for exploration. A perfect spot for an *apéro* (page 170), the constantly changing wine-by-the-glass menu is varied and affordable, and features a selection of whites, rosés, reds, and sparkling wines. If you're still hungry after an *assiette de fromage*, head across the street to the Siffleur's sister restaurant L'Ebauchoir (43 rue de Citeaux, 12th arrondissement) for a classic

French meal and the same extraordinary wine list.

Another newcomer to the natural wine scene is En Vrac (2 rue de l'Olive, 18th arrondissement). Making its début with a market stand at the neighboring Marché La Chapelle (or Marché de l'Olive, as locals call it), En Vrac started with a few barrels of natural wine and a selection of reusable bottles that customers could fill with the wine of their choice. In 2013, En Vrac moved to a brick and mortar space on the same block (2 rue de l'Olive, 18th arrondissement). The concept remains the same— bulk wine at affordable prices—but with the additional space En Vrac has expanded to sell a carefully selected collection of bottles as well as incorporate a small dining space and popular terrace in front, where locals enjoy natural wines and a sunny brunch.

If you're looking to make a soirée out of your natural wine experience, there are several natural wine bars and restaurants to choose from. Favorites include the sometimes rowdy and always convivial Le Garde Robe (41 rue de l'Arbre Sec, 1st arrondissement), where you can enjoy small plates and tapas and wines by the glass or bottle. La Buvette (67 rue Saint Maur, 11th arrondissement) specializes in carefully selected wines and simple yet delicious small plates made by owner Camille Fourmont, from quality ingredients. For a hearty meal on the quiet side of the Sacré Coeur, duck into Le Grand 8 (8 rue Lamarck, 18th arrondissement). This laid-back restaurant is popular with visiting natural winemakers, who will find many of their cohorts included on the menu. Meals are prepared with quality produce suited to the stellar wine list. Grab a table early at the Café de la Nouvelle Mairie (19 rue des Fossés Saint-Jacques, 5th arrondissement) and you can enjoy a cheese or

charcuterie plate with your wine. Pressure is on to dine or depart once the dinner service starts, but you won't regret staying for their simple meals inspired by seasonal ingredients.

AUTUMN RECIPES

APPETIZERS, SIDES, SALADS, AND SOUPS

SEASONAL CHEESE PLATE / ASSIETTE DE FROMAGE

There's nothing easier to prepare than a simple cheese plate. This carefully curated dish—served after the main dish and before (or in lieu of) dessert—is often one of the favorite courses among dinner guests who are happy to discover a wide array of cheeses selected by their host. In order to put together a classic cheese plate, there are a few guidelines to follow—but mostly the process involves having fun at your local *fromagerie* or the dairy section of your favorite store.

Chèvre at L'Alpage fromagerie near Marché d'Aligre.

Cheese will vary slightly from season to season, with the most noticeable differences being between the colder months of autumn and winter and the sunnier spring and summer seasons. Fresh spring cheeses will be young and made with the milk of grass-fed animals. Cows, goats, and sheep that graze in pastures during the warmer months will produce cheese that has a grassy, floral taste. If you are planning a cheese plate during this time, it is worth including one or two younger cheeses that will reflect the true taste of this season. Autumn and winter bring with them aged cheeses that have been becoming harder and sharper over the months. These cheeses can be very interesting, with an earthy quality that is unrivaled when truly well done.

When assembling your *assiette de fromage*, try to choose at least three to five cheeses—you don't want to overwhelm guests with choice, but variety is nice to have in order to compare and contrast tastes. Arrange cheese on your plate from mildest (young spring chèvre or a young *comté*) to strongest (blue cheese or any aged, sharp cheese)—this should be the order that guests eat them in, avoiding overcoming any subtle tastes with stronger ones.

As for pairing wine with your cheeses, there are many commonly held theories on how best to do so. Some say red should always be served with fromage, even though white wine can go perfectly well with many, if not all, cheeses. Others maintain that cheese should be served with the wine from their region, which seriously limits your creativity in the cheese department and is also not necessarily true. If you're lucky enough to have a good cheese vendor at your market, grocery store—or even your favorite wine bar—they will likely be able to suggest some bottles to pair with your cheese plate. Otherwise, choose a favorite bottle to go with your customized cheese collection and enjoy!

CHICKPEA PANCAKES / *SOCCA*

Socca is a laid-back southern starter and snack. It is often eaten tapas-style, with deep-fried zucchini flowers and fish. In Paris, socca can be hard to find; that's why there's always a line at Alain's stand at *Marché des Enfants Rouges* (page 10), where the friendly vendor prepares hot-off-the-griddle socca for eager eaters. Serve your socca fresh out of the oven, broken into jagged sections that guests can eat with their hands. Fresh ground black pepper is key to this recipe; socca should never be served without being given a few turns of the pepper mill first.

Ingredients

Makes 2–3 batches

1 cup (150 grams) chickpea flour
1 cup (240 mL) water
2 large pinches of fine sea salt
2½ tablespoons extra virgin olive oil
Fresh ground black pepper
Coarse sea salt (optional)

Preparation

Whisk together chickpea flour, water, salt, and olive oil in a large bowl. Cover bowl with a dish towel and let sit for at least one hour. Preheat oven to 400°F (200°C). Once oven is preheated, lightly brush a baking sheet with olive oil. Pour batter into the baking sheet, creating a thin, even layer. Bake for 10–15 minutes or until golden and crispy around the edges. Remove from baking sheet by scraping and breaking socca into jagged pieces with a spatula. Repeat until all the remaining batter is used, combining scraped socca onto one large plate. Top with fresh ground black pepper and coarse sea salt, if using. Serve immediately.

KRISTEN'S BRAISED BRUSSELS SPROUTS / *CHOUX DE BRUXELLES BRAISÉS*

This is one of *The Kale Project* (page 5) founder Kristen Beddard's wonderful recipes inspired by the cabbage family. Brussels sprouts arrive at the market at the end of autumn, bringing with them endless possibilities for preparation. This vegetable has always been one of my favorites and Kristen's method of lightly braising the brussels sprouts brings out their flavor while maintaining their nutritional benefits. This quick and easy recipe makes a perfect side dish to an autumn or winter meal.

Ingredients

Serves 4

4 tablespoons (55 grams) of salted butter

1 pound (280 grams) of brussels sprouts, halved

Dash of salt and pepper

2 medium shallots, thinly sliced

1 cup (240 mL) dry white wine

Preparation

Melt butter in large pan. Add halved brussels sprouts face down. Cook in butter on medium heat for 3–4 minutes. Add salt, pepper, shallots, and dry white wine. Cover and cook for 4 minutes. Stir lightly. Cover and cook on low heat for another 5–7 minutes. Serve immediately.

FISH SOUP / *SOUPE DE POISSON*

This recipe is not for the faint of heart. If you're squeamish about handling fish heads and fins, you may want to abstain. With that said, this is a fun and hands-on meal to make. I've often seen the least likely of dinner guests get excited about participating in the process, stewing fish heads then grinding them into a thick broth that makes a hearty and delicious soup and embraces fin-to-tail cuisine.

Fish soup is a specialty of Marseille, but is served around the country, with variations being embraced as far as Normandy and Brittany. Work with your fishmonger to put together a selection of seasonal fish that will make a delicious—and show stopping—fish soup. Good fish to include in the soup are red mullet, bream, and scorpion fish. Make sure to ask that the vendor guts and fillets the fish for you—that's tricky work! This soup is traditionally served with croutons that are topped with *Rouille* (page 32) and then sprinkled with grated Gruyère cheese.

Ingredients

Serves 4

4 carrots, peeled and cut into ½ slices

2 yellow potatoes, peeled and cubed

1 medium leek, cut into ½ slices

4 large tomatoes, chopped (or one 16 oz. canned tomatoes)

Preparation

Place carrots, potatoes, leek, tomatoes, and onion in a large stockpot and cover with water. Season with a dash of salt and pepper. Bring water to boil and then reduce to simmer. Cook for 5 minutes. Cut fish fillets into uniform-sized pieces, about 2 inches large. Add fish fillets and frames into the simmering water. Cover and cook for 30–45 minutes, until vegetables are tender and the fish

1 yellow onion, diced
2 garlic cloves, coarsely chopped
Water
Salt and pepper
2 pounds (1 kilo) fresh whole fish,
    such as red mullet, bream, and
    scorpion fish. This should be a
    mixture of both fillets (ask your
    fishmonger to fillet the fish for
    you if you don't know how to
    do it) and the frame (head, tail,
    fins, etc.) of the fish.

is cooked, and the flesh has fallen off the fish frames.

Remove stockpot from heat and use a slotted spoon to extract large pieces of fish frames from the broth; these can either be discarded or saved to make a lighter fish broth later. Transfer the boneless broth in batches to a hand mill and mill the stock into a large soup pot. Once all the stock has been liquefied, reheat in soup pot and serve hot with croutons, rouille, and grated Gruyère.

ROUILLE

Ingredients

Makes about 1 cup

1 egg yolk, room temperature

1 tablespoon Dijon mustard

2 cloves of garlic, crushed

¾ cup (180 mL) extra virgin olive
   oil

2 teaspoons of paprika

Preparation

Use a whisk to beat together egg yolk and Dijon
mustard until they emulsify, becoming pale yellow
with a thick consistency. Stir in crushed garlic.
Slowly add oil in a steady stream as you continue to
whisk to incorporate. Whisk until mayonnaise
thickens and all the oil is incorporated, about 1–2
minutes. If the sauce begins to get too thin, stop
adding oil. Stir in paprika. Refrigerate at least 30
minutes before serving.

HEARTY OVEN ROASTED ROOT VEGETABLES /
LÉGUMES RÔTIS AU FOUR

When I first started visiting Paris markets and asking farmers for recipes I was surprised to find that, contrary to my expectations, local producers rarely offered ideas for meat-heavy meals, leaning rather toward simple preparations that brought out the subtle and satisfying flavors of their homegrown produce. Thinking that the strenuous physical labor of farming would be fueled by a mostly carnivorous menu, I was happy to learn that most farmers are as happy as hippies to eat meat-free meals. So when I asked famed farmer *Joël Thiébault* (page 3) about his favorite autumn recipes I was not shocked when he suggested a simple roasted root vegetable dish that optimizes his fall harvest of heirloom and rare root vegetable varieties. You can use your favorite root vegetables or whatever you find at the market to make this hearty, seasonal side dish.

Ingredients

1 parsnip, coarsely chopped
1 medium celery root, cubed
2 turnips, coarsely chopped
2 carrots, cut into ½ slices
1 large yellow potato, cubed
2 garlic cloves, halved
Extra virgin olive oil
Salt and pepper
Optional: cubed beets, black radish cut into ½ inch pieces, chopped onions, chopped fennel, etc.

Preparation

Preheat oven to 400°F (200°C). Toss chopped vegetables and garlic in a large mixing bowl with olive oil until evenly coated. Arrange in one layer on a baking sheet. Season with a dash of salt and pepper. Place dish on top rack of oven and roast for 40–50 minutes, or until vegetables are golden on the outside and soft inside. Serve immediately.

QUICK LEEK SOUP /
VELOUTÉ DE POIREAUX

This is a sure-to-please recipe for the leek geek in your life. I'm often inspired to make this velvety soup when I see leaks poking out of shopping bags at my local market. Warming and nourishing, this quick soup is perfect for a chilly evening. Be sure to carefully wash leeks once you've removed the dark green leaves and cut the stalk in half; you will often find hidden dirt here, which a quick rinse with cold water will remove. The soup is traditionally finished with a touch of milk at the end to give it a creamier consistency, but you can omit milk and butter if you want to make the recipe dairy-free.

Ingredients

Serves 4
1 tablespoon (15 grams) salted butter
1 large onion, chopped
4 large leeks, each cut into ½ inch slices
2 medium yellow potatoes, cubed
Water
Salt and pepper to taste
¼ cup (60 mL) milk (optional)
Fresh parsley

Preparation

In a large pot, melt butter and sauté onion until translucent, about 3–5 minutes. Add leeks and cook until they sweat, another 3–5 minutes. Add potatoes and cover with water. Boil and then bring to a simmer on medium-high heat and cook until potatoes are tender (20–25 minutes). Transfer to a blender, or use an immersion blender to mix until puréed. Season with salt and pepper to taste. Slowly stir in milk, if using it, until you've reached a velvety consistency. Serve topped with fresh parsley.

KOHLRABI, APPLE, AND FENNEL SALAD / SALADE DE CHOUX-RAVE, POMME, ET FENOUIL

Kohlrabi is one of my favorite vegetables that I discovered upon moving to France. Beautiful purple and light green bulbs of *choux-rave* invade Paris markets in the autumn and stick around all season and into the colder months. Inspired by my love of raw fennel, I came up with this salad that celebrates the flavor of uncooked

kohlrabi, fresh fennel, and crisp autumn apples. If using a mandoline, cut ingredients into thin slices; otherwise, chop chunky slices for a heartier salad. Dress with a basic *Vinaigrette* (page 149) or a *Dijon Vinaigrette* (page 150).

Ingredients

Serves 4

2 medium heads kohlrabi, halved and thinly sliced

2 medium bulbs fennel, halved and thinly sliced

1 large Pink Lady or Red Delicious apple, thinly sliced

Vinaigrette (page 149)

Preparation

Toss kohlrabi, fennel, and apples slices with vinaigrette. Serve immediately or store in an airtight container in the refrigerator until ready to serve.

GARLICKY MUSHROOM SAUTÉ /
POÊLÉE DE CHAMPIGNONS À L'AIL

The French rarely go overboard with their garlic, but these mushrooms are the exception. This simple side dish is easy to make and flavorful, with a healthy dose of garlic and parsley. Be sure to let your mushrooms cook slowly on low heat, releasing their juices and bringing out their full flavor.

Ingredients

Serves 4

2 pounds (1 kilo) mushrooms (chanterelles, shiitake, or even button mushrooms will work)

2 tablespoons extra virgin olive oil

1 medium yellow onion, thinly sliced

1 medium shallot, thinly sliced

4 cloves garlic, crushed and chopped

2 tablespoons fresh parsley, chopped

Salt and pepper

Preparation

Under a thin stream of cold water, lightly wash mushrooms and remove their feet. Use a clean dish towel to dry the mushrooms, then cut them into uniform slices, about ¼ inch thick. Heat the olive oil on medium heat and sauté the onion and shallot until transparent, about 3–5 minutes. In the meantime, stir together garlic and parsley in a small bowl. Add mushrooms to the pan and cook, stirring occasionally, until they have given their juice and then the juice has been cooked off, 3–5 minutes. Add parsley and garlic and cook another 2–3 minutes, before the parsley begins to wilt. Remove from heat, season to taste with salt and pepper, and serve immediately.

SAUCE

HOLLANDAISE

When the chef at *La Pointe du Grouin* (page 79) told me that there was *"rien de plus simple"* ("nothing simpler!") than making a hollandaise sauce, I had my doubts. I knew for a fact that there were simpler things to do than making a hollandaise—like not making one, for example. But I was up to the challenge and am happy to say I only curdled a few eggs in the process of making my first hollandaise. Separating the fat from the butter (a process called clarifying) and making sure that the egg yolks never get too hot is key to this recipe, which makes up in delicious what it lacks in simplicity.

Ingredients

1½ sticks (175 grams) salted butter, clarified
4 egg yolks
Juice from ½ lemon
Salt

Preparation

Bring a large pot of water to boil. In a small saucepan, melt butter on low heat. As butter melts, the fat will rise to the top. Once totally melted, remove butter from heat and use a spoon to clarify the butter by skimming off the top layer of fat (some will fall to the bottom of the saucepan, but that's okay—remove as much as possible). In a medium pot, whisk together eggs yolks, lemon juice, and a pinch of salt. Rotate whisking the egg yolk mixture over your steaming pot of boiling water and away from heat. It is important that the egg yolks don't get too hot, or else they will curdle. The bottom of the pot should never be hot to the touch. Whisk until the egg yolks are firm and thick. Slowly drizzle melted butter into the egg yolk emulsion, constantly whisking and alternating between heat and no heat. Combine all the melted butter and continue to whisk until the sauce is creamy and pale yellow. If sauce thickens, whisk in a small amount of lemon juice. The sauce should be served as quickly as possible, as it will begin to thicken as it cools.

Whisking egg yolks for a hollandaise sauce.

MAINS

"PRINCE OF PARIS" GRILLED CHEESE SANDWICH WITH SIDE SALAD /
CROQUE MONSIEUR AU JAMBON DE PARIS

In a hidden workspace in the 11th arrondissement, Daniel Rochon works away, preparing the last jambon de Paris that is actually made in Paris. Stamped with an Eiffel Tower and bearing the name "Prince de Paris," this special ham is prepared without any additives or preservatives. Slices of Rochon's coveted jambon de Paris can be found at the *Terroirs d'Avenir* butcher shop (page 138) and select specialty shops in the city. The Croque Monsieur is an ageless classic, second only to the jambon-beurre sandwich as Paris's iconic lunch choice.

Ingredients

For each sandwich:
- 1–2 (15–30 grams) tablespoons salted butter
- 2 pieces of sliced white sandwich bread
- 1 slice of smoked ham
- 1 slice of young Gruyère
- ¼ cup (30 grams) grated Gruyère
- *Béchamel Sauce* (page 99) (optional)

Preparation

Preheat oven to 400°F (200°C). Butter one side of each slice of bread. Place a slice of ham on the buttered side of the bread, followed by the slice of Gruyère. Top each sandwich with second piece of bread, butter side down. If using béchamel, spread sauce evenly over the top slice and then sprinkle with grated Gruyère. If omitting béchamel, spread top slice of bread with butter and top with grated Gruyère.

Place directly on the highest rack in the oven and let grill for 10–12 minutes, or until cheese is melted and tops of sandwiches are golden brown.

Serve with a green salad tossed with homemade *Vinaigrette* (page 148).

A butcher slices ham at Terroirs d'Avenir, rue du Nil.

MUSHROOM RISOTTO WITH HONEY ROASTED FIGS /
RISOTTO AUX FIGUES RÔTIES

When my friends Forest, of 52 Martinis, and Melanie, of Gâteaux Mama, decided to raise the challenge of making a seasonal meal that revolved around early autumn figs, I jumped at the chance to participate and experiment with ideas for a main course. Mushrooms and figs are both exciting arrivals of the season, so I decided to bring the two together, making a simple mushroom risotto paired with honey roasted figs. This dish would be excellent with the addition of panfried scallops, but on its own, the savory risotto and subtle sweetness of the figs makes for an elegant vegetarian meal.

Ingredients

Serves 4

For the risotto:

2 tablespoons extra virgin olive
    oil
1 red onion, chopped
1 clove garlic, minced
2 cups (370 grams) arborio rice
½ cup (120 mL) full bodied red
    wine
4 cups (960 mL) vegetable broth
2 cups (150 grams) chopped
    fresh mushrooms (shiitake,
    chanterelle, or cèpes work well)
4 tablespoons Parmesan cheese

Preparation

Preheat oven to 425°F (220°C). In a large pot or casserole, heat olive oil on medium-high; once oil is heated, add onion and garlic and sauté until translucent, 3–5 minutes. Add rice and stir until coated in olive oil. Stir in red wine and cook until all the wine is absorbed. Continue stirring and add vegetable broth, in small batches, waiting until the rice absorbs all the liquid before adding more. After adding all but about a half cup of broth, add mushrooms and 3 tablespoons of Parmesan cheese (reserve the remaining parmesan to sprinkle on top of finished risotto before serving) and stir in well. If rice is undercooked after adding all the vegetable broth, add some water and continue cooking until done.

Melt butter in a small saucepan. While waiting for butter to melt, wash and pat dry figs, then cut them crosswise without cutting all the way through, just

For the figs:

2 tablespoons (30 grams) salted
    butter
8 fresh figs
Honey
3 large sprigs of fresh thyme

allowing them to open a bit. Place figs in an oven-safe dish, cut side up. Pour melted butter over figs, coating evenly. Spoon a small amount of honey into each fig. Break thyme sprigs into smaller pieces and insert a few branches into each fig. Roast in oven until softened, but still firm enough to keep their form, about 15–20 minutes.

Arrange figs next to risotto. Garnish with any remaining thyme sprigs and Parmesan and serve immediately.

VENISON PARMENTIER / PARMENTIER DE CHEVREUIL

This recipe was just what a crew of hungry harvesters needed after a long day in the vines during the *vendanges* (page 12). Private chef Yann Le Pollotec prepared this dish using meat from a deer that was hunted and cured on the grounds. Yann brought together the best of locally sourced ingredients and typical French cuisine to make a meal that our team savored while squeezed around Noëlla's dinner table. Another unforgettable harvest experience to add to the list.

Ingredients

Serves 6

2 pounds (800 grams) venison/ deer

3 carrots, chopped

2 leeks, chopped

3 turnips, chopped

4 tablespoons vegetable oil

4½ cups (300 grams) wild mushrooms (black trumpet or chanterelles work great)

¾ cup (100 grams) all purpose flour

¾ cup (180 mL) port wine

3½ cups (840 mL) veal (or beef) stock

1 sprig of fresh rosemary

2 dried bay leaves

1½ pound (600 grams) sweet potatoes, peeled

Preparation

Preheat oven to 400°F (200°C). Cut the meat into 1 inch (3 cm) squares. Place on a large plate and season with salt and pepper. Chop the carrots, leeks, and turnips into pieces that are about the same size as the meat. Heat vegetable oil in a deep pan until very hot and add the meat in batches, searing it on all sides until golden brown. Set aside. Lower heat to medium-high and cook the carrots, leeks, and turnips until they brighten, about 3–5 minutes. Add mushrooms and cook for about a minute, stirring frequently. Add the meat and flour and stir together while cooking for about 2 minutes, until the flour turns light brown. With a spoon, scrape anything that has stuck to the bottom of the pan. Add port and quickly bring to a boil while stirring. Add the stock, rosemary, and bay leaves and simmer, uncovered, for about an hour and a half on medium-low heat, until the meat is tender and the sauce has thickened.

1 pound (400 grams) Yukon Gold
   potatoes, peeled
¼ cup (50 grams) + 2 tablespoons
   salted butter
3 egg yolks
¼ cup (30 grams) grated Gruyère
   (optional)

In the meantime, cook the sweet potatoes and Yukon Gold potatoes in a pot of boiling salted water, until they can be easily pierced with a knife. Once fully cooked, drain potatoes well and mash them until smooth, adding ¼ cup (50 grams) salted butter as you go. Let cool to room temperature. Once cool, stir in egg yolks one by one until fully combined.

Cook your meat until tender, then transfer the stew to a large pan and cover it evenly with a layer of the mashed potatoes. Cover the potato layer with 2 tablespoons salted butter, cut into small squares. If adding cheese, top with grated Gruyère. Place in oven and cook for 30 minutes, or until the mash is golden brown. Serve immediately.

THREE CHEESE FONDUE /
FONDUE SAVOYARDE

In one of my early Paris apartments, I lived by a friendly *fromager* who was kind enough to grate pounds of cheese for my yearly Christmas fondue party. Grating all your fondue cheese is probably the most challenging part of making a fondue; the rest is just a question of melting and stirring, making this an ideal recipe for the beginner chef or a small city kitchen. Every year in that apartment in the 18th arrondissement, my friends were invited to squeeze around a crowded coffee table in my tiny living room and enjoy a fun and cozy holiday meal.

Fondue pots tend to be small and this delicious fondue will be devoured quickly, so be prepared to make two batches of fondue; the recipe below is enough for two batches. You can halve the measurements if you are making fondue for four or fewer people.

Ingredients

Serves 6

2 garlic cloves

2 cups (480 mL) dry white wine

2 pounds (1 kilo) cheese, equal parts Beaufort, Comté, and Tomme de Savoie, grated

4–5 day-old baguettes, cut into cubes

Preparation

Cut a garlic clove in half. Rub the inside of the fondue pot with the garlic, and leave the half-clove at the bottom of the pot. Heat the fondue pot on medium until warm, 3–5 minutes. Add 1 cup (240 mL) of white wine to the heated pot and bring to a slow simmer. Add half of the cheese mixture in small handfuls, stirring consistently with a wooden spoon. Keep adding cheese until fully melted. Be sure to maintain a liquid consistency, so the fondue falls in ribbons from your wooden spoon. If too thick, add additional white wine. Serve hot, with bowls of cubed bread.

GOLDEN SWISS CHARD GRATIN / GRATIN DE BLETTES

This is a simple and nourishing autumn dinner, easy to prepare after work and a great way to use the ubiquitous Swiss chard that arrives with the changing of the leaves. Bake until golden and bring a little autumn sunshine into your evening!

Ingredients

Serves 4
4–5 stalks, Swiss chard, chopped
Béchamel (page 99)
1 cup (120 grams) grated Gruyère
Salt and pepper

Preparation

Preheat oven to 400°F (200°C). Wash and dry each stalk of Swiss chard. Remove the ends of Swiss chard stalks if dirty and then chop each stalk into thirds. Arrange Swiss chard in a large baking dish. Pour béchamel sauce over the Swiss chard. Top with grated Gruyère, salt, and pepper and bake for 20 minutes or until golden brown.

DESSERTS

PÂTE BRISÉE

For years I watched French friends whip up pie crusts for a quick quiche or tart so naturally that it seemed like something anyone could do. On an extended quiche kick one winter, I decided to try to make my own dough from scratch. Thus began my long and exasperating struggle with pâte brisée. Turns out the French are either born with innate mastery of dough, or my friends just had a flair for the *patisserie*; in any case, it took many attempts on my part before I could make a tart from scratch.

The trick with this recipe is not to overwork the dough, allowing for the water to be absorbed by the flour and butter mixture. The result is a flaky, versatile dough that works with both savory and sweet dishes. You can buy premade dough, of course, but there is little in life that rivals the feeling of satisfaction that comes with making your own.

Ingredients

Makes enough dough for one 10-inch (25 cm) pie tin

2 cups (240 grams) all purpose flour

1 teaspoon fine sea salt

1 cup (225 grams) chilled butter, cut into ½ inch (2 cm) cubes

½ cup (120 mL) ice water

Preparation

Mix flour and salt together, in a bowl or a food processor, on low speed. Add butter and mix until fully combined. If using a food processor, mix slowly and no longer than 15 seconds; if combining by hand, mix together for no longer than a minute, just enough to integrate butter. It is okay if there are some lumps in the dough; these will disappear between the rolling out and baking. Slowly add ice water while combining or mixing by hand again. Do not work the dough longer than another 15–30 seconds with a food processor or 1 minute by hand. Gather dough together with hands—it can be a bit crumbly, but should stick when pressed together. Form a disc with the dough, about ½ inch (2 cm) thick and 4–5 inches (11 cm) in diameter. Wrap in wax paper and refrigerate for at least one hour.

Once chilled, remove dough from refrigerator and allow it to come to room temperature. If the dough is too cold when rolling out it will tear, and if it is too warm it will stick to the rolling pin and countertop. When the dough is just slightly sticky, roll it out on a floured surface with a floured rolling pin Roll to desired size, flipping over as necessary. Make sure dough has a uniform thickness and that it corresponds to the size of the pie tin.

APPLESAUCE / COMPOTE DE POMMES

Ingredients

Makes about 1 ½ cups (225 grams)
6 Golden Delicious or Jonagold
  apples, peeled and cored
½ cup (120 mL) water
½ cup (100 grams) unrefined
  sugar
¼ teaspoon vanilla extract

Preparation

Heat an empty pan on medium-high heat for 5 minutes. While heating pot, cut peeled and cored apples into equal size pieces, about 1 inch (2 cm). Add apples, water, sugar, and vanilla to heated pot. Cover and reduce heat and cook for 20–25 minutes, until apples become soft. Remove from heat and use a wooden spoon or fork to crush apples about 3–5 minutes, or until they reach desired consistency—it should be chunky if using to make an *Apple Tarte* (page 52) or can be made smoother and prepared as a *Yogurt Parfait* (page 158) by using an immersion blender.

PICARDIE APPLE TARTE / TARTE AUX POMMES

Ingredients

Serves 4–6 people
Pâte Brisée (page 48)
1½ cups (225 grams) *Applesauce*
(page 50)
6–8 Granny Smith or Golden
Delicious apples, peeled and
cored

Preparation:

Preheat oven to 375°F (190°C). Line a shallow 10-inch (25 cm) round pie tin with pâte brisée. Cut off any excess crust around the edges and use fingers to mold crust to fit the perimeter of the pie tin. Spread a layer of apple compote on the bottom of the pie tin, distributing evenly. Slice apples into uniform size pieces and use them to create a spiral design starting from the center of the tin and expanding outward until all space is covered (the apple slices can overlap a bit). Bake 25–30 minutes, until dough is cooked through and apples are golden. Serve immediately, with *Crème Anglaise* (page 56) if desired.

EMPEROR NORTON'S SNICKERDOODLES

I challenge you to find anything cuter than the French pronunciation of "Snickerdoodle," a word that has recently entered the French lexicon thanks to *Emperor Norton* (page 8) and their cookie crusade. A perfect pairing to a chai tea at Loustic, Omid and Alannah's snickerdoodles are a favorite among Parisians, who are eagerly expanding their knowledge of American baked goods to go beyond chocolate chip cookies and cupcakes.

Ingredients

Makes about 10 cookies

For cookies:

1 cup (220 grams) softened salted butter
1½ cups (300 grams) unrefined sugar
1 medium egg
2½ cups (330 grams) all purpose flour
2 teaspoons cream of tartar
1 teaspoon baking soda
½ teaspoon salt

For spice mix:

2 tablespoons ground star anise
1 tablespoon ground cinnamon
1 tablespoon ground cloves
1 tablespoon ground coriander
¼ cup (50 grams) unrefined sugar

Preparation

Preheat oven to 350°F (180°C). Cream together butter and sugar. Mix in egg then add in flour, cream of tartar, baking soda, and salt, mixing with a spatula or spoon until mostly combined and then finishing with the mixer. Shape dough into ten uniform sized balls and chill in refrigerator for at least 30 minutes. Remove from refrigerator and roll dough balls in the spice mixture, coating each one evenly with spices. Bake on wax paper–lined sheets for 12–14 minutes. Cool completely before serving or storing in an airtight container.

FOREST FORAGED WALNUT CAKE / GÂTEAU AUX NOIX

I made this cake in late autumn during the pruning season at Noëlla Morantin and Laurent Saillard's vineyards in the Loire (page 12). Walnuts that had been foraged in the nearby forest gave the cake a little local flavor. A perfect dessert to end an autumnal meal, this cake pairs pleasantly with a cup of coffee or tea and can be served on its own, or with a drizzle of *Crème Anglaise* (page 56) for an added touch of sweetness.

Ingredients

1 stick (110 grams) softened butter

¾ cup (150 grams) sugar

3 eggs, white and yolks separated

1 teaspoon vanilla

⅓ cup (40 grams) flour

1½ cups (200 grams) walnuts, coarsely chopped

1 pinch of salt

Preparation

Preheat oven to 400°F (210°C). Butter and flour an 8-inch (20 cm) circular cake pan. Cream together butter and sugar. Stir in egg yolks one by one. Stir in vanilla. Fold flour into egg mixture, followed by walnuts. In a separate bowl, whip egg whites until they begin to froth up, then add a pinch of salt and continue beating until they become fluffy with soft peaks. Mix ⅓ of the egg whites into the batter, and then fold remaining egg whites in batches into the batter, until fully combined. Pour batter into cake pan. Bake for 20–30 minutes, or until a toothpick comes out of the cake clean. Serve warm, drizzled with crème anglaise if desired.

CUSTARD / CRÈME ANGLAISE

Ingredients

1 cup (240 mL) skim milk
1 teaspoon vanilla extract
¼ cup (50 grams) sugar
2 egg yolks

Preparation

In a small saucepan over medium-high heat, bring milk and vanilla extract to a slow boil. In a separate bowl, whisk together sugar and egg yolks. Once milk begins to steam, remove from heat and stir in egg yolk and sugar mixture. When the milk has reached an even liquid consistency, return to medium heat and keep stirring until the cream thickens and coats your spoon or spatula.

WINTER

A rather poetic friend once said to me, during a particularly gray day when clouds had eclipsed the city's skies and rain overcame us, "I love it when Paris is in one of her moods." Mood-related or not, winter weather in Paris can change overnight or even several times a day. Selection at the market shifts just as quickly, with every visit to your local marché bearing witness to the inevitable transition from the cornucopia of autumn vegetables to the more restricted choice of the winter harvest.

Winter is a season of dinner parties among friends and family, with loved ones convening in cozy apartments and spending many hours *à table*. The shorter days mean that apartment building stairways start to smell of sautéing onions and garlic early in the day as Parisians prepare hearty meals, taking their time to enjoy the warmth of a home-cooked meal, no matter what mood the city may be in.

As the last leaves fall from the trees and the streets become illuminated with Christmas lights and decorations, Parisians greet the festive season by indulging in special occasion menu items, such as champagne, oysters, and rich chocolate cakes, making this a delicious and decadent time to be in the city.

In Season: apples, beets, endives, brussels sprouts, cabbage, carrots, celery, onions, parsnips, potatoes, shallots, shell beans, sunchokes, turnips, winter squash

MARCHÉ DAUMESNIL

BOULEVARD DE REUILLY, 75012
M° DAUMESNIL (LINE 6 AND 8)
OPEN: TUESDAY AND FRIDAY, 7:00 A.M.–2:30 P.M.

Local producers abound at Marché Daumesnil, a treasure trove of product-eurs from nearby farms. This expansive market counts a wide selection of farmers from the Île-de-France region as well as a choice of vendors selling organic vegetables and baked goods. Veer away from the aisles of textiles and stay on the odd-numbered side of boulevard de Reuilly in order to find the serious veggie vendors.

Philippe Flamand sells a selection of baby greens and mushrooms that are grown in Melun (forty miles from Paris) while Fabrice Guilchet, located in the nearby Essone region, sells a mixture of his own homegrown produce along with some nonseasonal outsiders that he brings to the market. Jean-Luc Dormoy sells colorful cauliflower and a variety of lettuce, cabbage, gourds, and root vegetables in winter. All produce is grown on his farm which is located only fifteen miles from Paris. The Dormoy stand overflows with pumpkins and seasonal squash throughout the season. Favorites include the small speckled Kabocha squash and the Fairytale pumpkin variety (which looks like it jumped off a page of *Cinderella*).

Mme. Dormoy always has a serving suggestion for her fruits and vegetables, and is happy to share it with whoever takes the time to ask. Pick up any pumpkin variety and she will tell you exactly what to do with it. Transactions at the Dormoy stand often end with a wink and a smile as you are sent off to experiment with your fresh produce and new recipe.

PARIS'S SPECIALTY COOKWARE SHOPS

Shopping for cooking supplies and accessories in Paris is just as fun as scouring the city's markets for fresh ingredients. A selection of favorite shops is home to French-made products and kitchen essentials. During the holiday season, G Detou (58 rue Tiquetonne, 2nd arrondissement) is filled with boxes of chocolates and other standards for Christmas and New Year's parties. Featured chocolatiers include Normandy-based Michel Cluizel and Southern France native Chocolat Weiss. Regional French products such as Calissons d'Aix from Provence and sea salt caramels from Brittany bring loyal customers to this cozy boutique, but it is the more foreign fare that brings expats from around the city.

Hard-to-find ingredients such as maple syrup, cranberries, and elusive baking supplies, such as baking powder and sprinkles, are coveted by bakers

seeking to recreate North American specialties. This shop surely lives up to its name, which translates to "I have everything." Shelves are heavily stocked with a variety of sugars, bulk nuts and dried fruits, food coloring, specialty flours, and cake decorating supplies. The friendly staff is knowledgeable and happy to help make your baking plans a reality, often sneaking to the back of the shop and coming back with products that aren't stocked in their tiny showroom. Here you will also find a large selection of baking chocolate, perfect for your *Queen of Sheba Cake* (page 115) or a *Mont Salève Chocolate Imperial Stout Cake* (page 109).

A second G Detou located next door to the original boutique serves as a deli counter with largely French and Italian products such as sardines, preserved vegetables, and specialty mustards. You can also find vacuum-packed goods ranging from smoked salmon to sausages and regional specialties such as quenelles, a sort of meat dumpling popular in Lyon, all of which make unique souvenirs to bring home.

Made-in-France linens at La Tresorie.

The twin A. Simon boutiques, also in the Etienne Marcel neighborhood (48 rue Montmartre, 2nd arrondissement), are fun places to browse for both amateur and professional chefs. Made-in-France cookware brands such as De Boyer, Stuab, and Le Creuset share shelf space with gorgeous copper pots and professional cutlery sets. Here you will also find a large selection of mandolines and high-grade kitchen tools such as hefty garlic presses costing 47 euro, and similarly-priced vegetable peelers and graters. The shop caters more to the professional chef and restaurant owner, with a section for typical bistrot blackboards and multi-colored markers to write out a changing *carte du jour.* In A. Simon's second boutique, you will find a large selection of products for the home. Stemware, flatware, and simple porcelain serving-ware make charming French touches to your kitchen or dining room. You can also find molds for making *Madeleines* (page 196) and soufflé dishes for a *Rainy Day Cheese Soufflé* (page 108), along with a wide selection of wine accessories, from classy glasses to sophisticated screw pulls to sleeves for keeping wine cool (or hidden while hosting a blind tasting).

The sense of history is palpable at E. Dehillerin (18–20 rue Coquillière, 1st arrondissement), which has been around for 190 years and seems to have barely changed in that time. The shop's walls are largely lined with pegged boards, reminiscent of Julia Child's kitchen, a former regular customer at this shop. Floor-to-ceiling sturdy wooden shelves make up aisles of pans, pots, and skillets. Ogle the wide selection of whisks and imagine the fresh batches of *Aioli* (page 146) or *Béchamel* (page 99) you could use them to whip up. Here you will find a knife for every culinary task and a dish for every meal.

The clientele is largely professional—on a recent visit, I overheard a customer ask the question, "Can I use this knife to carve a pheasant?" (The response: "You're the second person to ask me that today.") But that doesn't mean beginner chefs can't enjoy a stroll around this store and the living culinary history it presents. Tourists often speak in a whisper while wandering the aisles, unconsciously showing respect for what truly feels like hallowed

Friendly service at Café Smögås.

gourmet ground. If you're looking to take a small piece of history home, grab a French-made Opinel paring knife or vegetable peeler.

A more modern approach to housewares is found at La Tresorie (11 rue Chateau d'Eau, 10th arrondissement). Roughly a third of all the products at La Tresorie are made in France and 90 percent are of European origin. Here you will find high quality, durable products at reasonable prices. A selection of typically French cotton tea towels and charming linen napkins and place mats make great gifts or settings for your next homemade French meal. They also carry a wide variety of French-specific cooking utensils, such as a crêpe spreader, special cheese knives, and darling L'Econome peelers and paring knives. Continuing with the minimalist Scandinavian-inspired style of the store, La Tresorie is attached to a Swedish restaurant called Café Smörgås, where you can snack on open-faced sandwiches and perk up with a cup of coffee from *Belleville Brulerie* (page 86).

MARCHÉ ALÉSIA

RUE DE LA GLACIÈRE 75013
M° GLACIÈRE (LINE 6)
OPEN: WEDNESDAY AND SATURDAY, 7 A.M.–2:30 P.M.

Where the rue de la Santé and rue de la Glacière converge, you will find Marché Alésia, a small market in a sleepy corner of the 13th arrondissement. While this part of Paris is usually visited for the bars in the Butte aux Cailles neighborhood or the authentic Chinese eateries that orbit the Place d'Italie, Marché Alésia merits a visit as well.

The market, which is tucked into a tree-lined street, is recognizable from afar by its striped circus tents and streams of lights. Walk about halfway down and you'll see a line of people waiting for freshly harvested fruits and vegetables that come from Isabelle and Daniel Behuret's farm. Located in Montlhéry, a mere twenty miles from Paris, the Behurets grow a selection of cabbage and lettuce varieties that are picked on the morning of the market.

THE NEW WAVE OF PARIS MARKETS

In addition to the numerous open-air and covered markets in Paris, some of which date back over four hundred years, a new wave of markets is sprouting up around the city. These markets embrace the "eat local" mentality and strive to put consumers in direct contact with the people who grow their food. Two outstanding newcomers to the market scene are Marché sur L'Eau and La Ruche Qui Dit Oui, both of which work with nearby farms to bring fresh produce to the city.

Marché sur L'Eau may have the most creative approach to transporting produce from the Seine and Marne region (forty miles from Paris) to La Rotonde in the 10th arrondissement. In lieu of using the equivalent ten trucks to freight the goods to the capital, Marché sur L'Eau brings its booty in by boat, which travels along the Canal de l'Ourcq and stops at three distribution points along the way. Parisians and visitors can stop by the market on

Tuesdays and early Saturday afternoons, where they can either purchase the vegetables of their choice or pick up a *panier*, or basket, that has been pre-ordered through their subscription program.

La Ruche Qui Dit Oui counts on farmers to bring their produce to the point of sale themselves. Designated sites known as *ruches*, or beehives, are scattered across the city and maintained by local volunteers. Farmers and consumers come together at these rendezvous locations to collect the locally grown products that they have ordered online in advance. A compelling mixture of both market and CSA (Community Supported Agriculture), La Ruche Qui Dit Oui allows shoppers to prepay and anticipate their purchases, but also have direct contact with the person who grew them.

While Paris's network of outdoor food markets is vast and well-organized, people with standard working hours or with no time to go to the market in the morning often miss out on having a hands-on market experience. La Ruche Qui Dit Oui and Le Marché Sur l'Eau bring the market back into people's lives and reignite a passion for shopping for produce and artisanal products close to home.

Another way that city dwellers can develop a relationship with local producers is by enrolling in an AMAP (Association pour le Maintien d'une Agriculture Paysanne). Similar to CSA networks in the United States, AMAPs connect members with a local farmer, who delivers a fresh crop of seasonal vegetables to the city every week. Enrolling in an AMAP not only involves a regular delivery of farm-fresh fruits and vegetables, but also entails payment for weekly deliveries up front and in advance, meaning members must weather whatever storms or misfortunes may befall their farmer. Temperature shifts, insect attacks, storms, etc. will have an effect on what you'll find in your AMAP basket that week. Members accept the varying quantity and quality of the produce as a sign of solidarity with their producer, and an understanding of the hard work and challenges of independent agriculture. Members can also get to know their farmers better by visiting the farm and volunteering to get their hands dirty and help out on the land. AMAPs not only bring neighborhood communities together, but they also extend that sense of community to the countryside, bringing farm and city that much closer.

MARCHÉ D'ALIGRE

RUE D'ALIGRE, 75012
Mº LEDRU-ROLLIN (LINE 8)
OPEN: TUESDAY–SUNDAY, 7:30 A.M.–1:30 P.M.

There are no farmers at the Marché d'Aligre, making it a disappointing destination if you're looking for fresh, local produce. Though the carefully curated selection of seasonal produce at Gilles Flahaut's stand—which is mostly sourced from France and reflects his knowledge of interesting vegetable varieties—is worth checking out, the true treasures lie on the outskirts of the market. The Marché couvert Beauvau, located next door to the outdoor Aligre market, is home to specialty vendors that specialize in regional and artisanal goods. Italian cheeses, dried fish from Africa, and beers from

around the world come together under the ancient wooden rafters of this former hay market. Standout booths include Sur les Quais, purveyor of organic olive oils, spices, chocolate, and other specialty ingredients. If you're in need of a snack or an afternoon *goûter* stop at Jojo&co, where delicate lemon bars, cookies, and airy little cakes are freshly baked and difficult to pass up.

After stocking up at the indoor market, visit the shops along the perimeter of Marché d'Aligre, which doubles as an all-day flea market (don't hesitate to browse the selection of inexpensive bakeware and used vinyls of *chanson française*). The prize for most charming—and space-optimizing—boutique is the tiny La Graineterie du Marché (8 place d'Aligre, 12th arrondissement). Packed with bins of bulk dried fruits, grains, beans, and spices, this shop is peppered with surprises—from reasonably priced vintage cookware and kitchen accessories to practical homeware such as dish towels and seeds for your windowsill or balcony herb garden. A great spot to shop year-round, this shop is particularly tempting in the winter months, when a dried peach

or some warm spices do wonders to break up the root vegetable and cold weather blues that have a habit of hitting us all.

Next try the cheese at L'Alpage (15 rue d'Aligre, 12th arrondissement), where the knowledgeable fromager's passion for cheese is contagious. From aged comté to moldy chèvre, this shop has everything you need to put together a *Seasonal Cheese Plate* (page 24) or make a *Rainy Day Cheese Soufflé* (page 108). Be sure to check out the selection of fresh creams, cheese, and yogurt that are great for the following day's breakfast. Certain cheeses can also be vacuum-packed on site, assuring they're ready for an international flight home.

Before leaving Marché d'Aligre, make a stop at Les Chocolats d'Aligre (13 rue d'Aligre, 12th arondissement). Ocean and Thierry, who make up the shop's friendly staff, work with France's most accomplished chocolatiers, bringing together a selection that mixes exciting surprises and impeccable classics in the world of French chocolate. Select a few favorites to taste with a coffee or put together a box of chocolates to take home and share with friends.

LA CUCINA DI TERRESA:
FRENCH ITALIAN FUSION À LA CALIFORNIENNE

I wouldn't appreciate the Marché d'Aligre the way I do if it weren't for Terresa Murphy, founder of La Cucina di Terresa, who was kind enough to give me a private tour of the market and was the first person to take me to La Graineterie.

Terresa is a great guide, not just for markets, but all things gastronomic. Her understanding of French wine and passion for Italian cuisine are the driving force behind the cooking classes she hosts in her home, adapting each session to the desires and size of the group, with recipes that bring together regional Italian cuisine and an emphasis on vegetables and a vegetarian diet. Her love of *légumes* has its origins in her early days of cooking in San Francisco, which she called home before moving to France in 1996. Terresa offers the opportunity to create simple yet wholesome and nourishing meals with locally sourced ingredients. Terresa's kitchen, which resembles a cabinet of curiosities, is decked out with dangling pots and pans, mason jars filled with herbs and spices, mills, mortars and pestles, and much, much more.

After spending a few hours sipping and snacking and preparing a wonderful home-cooked meal, guests pull up a chair at a cozy table and enjoy a bottle of perfectly paired natural wines. Terresa's palette is as trustworthy as it gets when it comes to pairing wines with her genre of vegetarian cuisine, and her love of the Loire Valley and its various grape varieties shines in her choice of Sauvignon Blanc, Chenin, and Pineau d'aunis. Terresa is so enamored by the Loire and the kindred spirits she's met there that she started offering a full day tour of the region. Guests are guided as they visit local winemakers, taste their wines (all natural, of course), take part in a cooking class in a rustic setting, and enjoy a meal among new friends.

THE RUE DU NIL: LOCAL LOVER'S LANE

On a shady side street in the 2nd arrondissement a gathering of new neighbors has subtly transformed the way Paris shoppers buy local. Chef Gregory Marchand was the first to install himself on the sleepy street when he opened Frenchie (5 rue du Nil, 2nd arrondissement), which quickly became one of the city's most sought-after reservations. Two years later the chef opened Frenchie Wine Bar (6 rue du Nil, 2nd arrondissement) across the street, a no-reservations option that had devotees lined up outside the door up to an hour before opening time. The most recent addition to Marchand's Frenchie empire, Frenchie To Go, is also on the rue du Nil and functions as a popular deli counter and lunch spot for locals and gourmands alike. Thanks partly to Marchand, in the span of a couple of years, the rue du Nil became a veritable destination for visitors from around the world.

The renown of the street has increased with the opening of *Terroirs d'Avenir* (7 rue du Nil, 2nd arrondissement) in 2013. Founded by business school buddies Alexandre Drouand and Samuel Nahon, Terrroirs d'Avenir began by developing relationships with small-scale producers in order to bring high quality, unique ingredients to Paris chefs.

With the brick and mortar shop, Terroirs d'Avenir has expanded to serve shoppers who want access to the same great ingredients they find at restaurants such as Frenchie, Verjus, Spring, and other local-leaning restaurants (page 77). Preserving specialties from the Île-de-France region is paramount in the business plan, and Terroirs d'Avenir remains one of the few shops where you will find vegetable varieties such as the choux de Pontoise and other local specialties from nearby agricultural regions including Cergy and Argenteuil.

In addition to fresh, local produce, the original store is also stocked with natural wines, locally brewed beers, and a selection of cheese. Additional

outposts of Terroirs d'Avenir, located just across the street, now include a butcher and fishmonger, both sourcing from the finest producers in France.

The latest rue du Nil tenant, L'Arbre à Café (10 rue du Nil, 2nd arrondissement), brings with it some of the city's most delicious fresh roasted coffee. Owner Hippolyte Courty sells organic and biodynamically farmed single-origin beans from small producers in India, Columbia, Brazil, and other coffee-growing regions of note. The store also sells a selection of the sublime Claudio Corallo chocolates.

Marché Place des Fêtes

PLACE DES FÊTES, 75019
Mº PLACE DES FÊTES (LINE 7BIS AND 11)
OPEN: TUESDAY, FRIDAY, AND SUNDAY, 7:00 A.M.–2:30 P.M.

Located in the culturally rich Belleville neighborhood of the 19th arrondissement, Marché Place des Fêtes attracts a diverse crowd of shoppers. The charming place squeezes in as many stands as possible, with vendors selling everything from yarn to cooking supplies to organic produce.

Marché Place des Fêtes is home to two local farmers, Guy Barrais and Patrick Messant. Both from the Seine-et-Marne in Île-de-France, these farmers see crowds flock to their stands three times a week, as they arrange wooden crates of fresh, seasonal produce. On Sundays be ready to stand in line for quite some time before getting your chance to choose from the root vegetables, apples, and cabbage that abound during the winter months. While waiting in line, have no shame in eavesdropping in the hopes of recipe

inspiration, as talk of a homemade pot-au-feu or winter stew keeps you warm while you wait to fill up your market basket. Both Guy Barrais and Patrick Messant can also be found at Marché Ordener (rue Ordener, 18th arrondissement).

PARIS'S LOCAL-LEANING RESTAURANTS

A regional initiative to purpose labels indicating local-leaning restaurants (page 81) is a step in the right direction for designating quality ingredients in the city's kitchens, but as of yet no compulsory certification has been proposed on a national level. It therefore falls to the consumer to deduce which Paris restaurants will live up to the standards of hungry locavores.

Luckily, there are several frequently updated online guides aimed at pointing Parisians in the right direction. The trustworthy French site Le Fooding is a guide that attempts to take the stuffiness out of French food writing. Restaurants of all types are reviewed here, with frequent profiles of chefs and interviews with famous French personalities about their favorite restaurants and *bonnes adresses*. For anglophones, the culinary touchstone when it comes to deciding where to dine is undoubtedly Paris by Mouth. Here you will find reviews and articles written by well-loved Paris food writers

(including founders Meg Zimbeck and Alexander Lobrano, and guest writers such as Clotilde Dusoulier) who write up recent openings and add them to the site's exhaustive list of well-loved Paris restaurants. Nods are given in the review notes to restaurants that embrace market-based cooking, "prestige ingredients," vegetarian options, and natural wines.

The list of restaurants preparing locally sourced fresh, seasonal ingredients is growing and there is plenty of choice for places to dine in Paris. Terroir Parisien (20 rue Saint-Victor, 5th arrondissement) is chef Yannick Alléno's restaurant, inspired by a tasting menu of the same name that Alléno served in the prestigious restaurant of the Hotel Meurice. Terroir Parisien is a step back from the high prices and haute cuisine of the Hotel Meurice, embracing a bistrot-style dining experience, where menu items such as onion soup, stuffed cabbage, and a simple *croque monsieur* are inspired by ingredients that have been traditionally grown or cultivated in the Paris region.

Nico Alary and Sarah Mouchot of Holybelly.

When Braden Perkins and Laura Adrian opened up their wine bar Verjus (47 rue Montpensier, 1st arrondissement) in 2011, their idea was to pair quality wines with foods that were foreign to the French palate. Small plate tapas-style dining was served à la carte and took the form of fried chicken, french fries, and homemade ketchup. A restaurant opened upstairs shortly after the wine bar began to overflow, becoming an extension of the bar's spirit of adventure and discovery. Chef Braden Perkins works with Normandy farmer Annie Bertin, to source ingredients that are locally grown and unfailingly fresh. Bertin's seasonal ingredients and heirloom varieties shine in Perkins's inventive recipes, which are featured as part of the eight-course tasting menu that can be adapted upon request to suit special dietary needs.

The frenzied success of Holybelly (19 rue Lucien Sampaix, 10th arrondissement) is no surprise to ex-pats in Paris, who have been longing for a cozy space to enjoy a late morning breakfast along with good coffee. In addition to comfort foods such as pancakes, bacon, and eggs, chef Sarah Mouchot serves more nuanced *plats du jour* inspired by her travels with partner Nico Alary and, most of all, what's best and in season. A typical winter menu will include classic favorites such as eggs, bacon, and hash browns along with more adventurous offerings such as *Beef Cheek Stew with Fried Polenta and Salad* (page 100).

Holybelly's back wall is decked out with an enormous chalkboard that announces what is in season and the origins of all the ingredients used in house. Dedicated to preparing innovative food with fresh ingredients, Sarah and her original co-chef Lise Kvan quickly found an eager audience of devout diners, which included ex-pats as well as natives. Nico Alary greets guests with a smile as he prepares filter coffees and cappuccinos and tries to find open seats for hungry crowds. The smiles and satisfying meals served at Holybelly are the secret to its success as one of the most welcoming restaurants in the city.

Don't be intimidated by owner Thierry Breton's wacky system of currency at La Point du Grouin (8 rue de Belzunce, 10th arrondissement)—once it's been explained how to exchange euro for the restaurant's signature tokens, called *grouins*, you're in for a treat. Super affordable lunch and dinner options are comprised of menu items made from the freshest ingredients and prepared in-house, including the bread, which is worth the trip on its own. Orders are placed at the bar and the arrival of your meal is announced over a loudspeaker by the staff. The self-service approach to dining may sound impersonal, but rest assured that the welcome is warm and the service friendly and imbued with an eagerness to share information regarding the well-thought-out and locally sourced menu. Breton's neighboring restaurant, Chez Casimir (6 rue de Belzunce, 10th arrondissement), has one of the city's most filling and French brunches and the added bonus of a self-serve wine cellar stocked with a wide selection of stellar natural wines.

With fresh fish from *Terroirs d'Avenir* (page 138), veggies from farmer *Joël Thiébault* (page 3) and locally roasted coffee from *L'Arbre à Café* (page 75), Le Bon Georges (45 rue Saint-Georges, 9th arrondissement) proudly publicizes the provenance of its locally sourced ingredients. While on board with the international farm-to-table trend, Le Bon Georges remains true to its French origins (meat is only served prepared one way—rare—as the French like it) and is the quintessential French restaurant in all but one regard: the extremely friendly service. Diners are greeted by the restaurant's patron and guided through the menu with care and patience. This neighborhood restaurant attracts locals and travelers alike, making for an enchanting crossroads of cultural and culinary discovery.

THE LABEL DEBATE: FACT CHECKING *FAIT MAISON*

While a growing number of restaurants are dedicated to sourcing fresh, local ingredients and preparing everything on site (page 77), in France there is a real threat of industrial, preserved foods taking over the daily menu at your neighborhood restaurant. Efforts to increase awareness of the poor quality of food in some dining establishments are helping to educate diners and apply pressure to restaurant owners. A *fait maison* ("homemade") label attesting to the fact that food is prepared in-house was created and implemented by the French government in July 2014. The effectiveness and authenticity of this label, which allows for frozen foods to be considered as part of a homemade meal, is debatable, but some see it as a step in the right direction.

While the government continues to consider how to best protect the country's culinary tradition at the national level, local legislators have come up

with their own solutions. In the Île-de-France department, a special brand called "Saveurs d'Île-de-France" was created to designate products that are grown or produced in the area surrounding Paris. Taking this local pride a step further, the brand created the *Des produits d'ici, Cuisinés Ici* (Products from Here, Prepared Here) label, which restaurants can opt to display for customers, guaranteeing that local ingredients are used as much as possible and that everything the restaurant serves is prepared in-house. Over fifty restaurants in the Île-de-France region sport the "Des produits d'ici, Cuisinés ici" label, of which forty-two are in Paris. So if you find  yourself strolling in one of the city's gastronomic dead-zones (think anywhere near a large tourist attraction), keep your eye out for *des produits d'ici*. Participating restaurants like La Bonne Franquette (2 rue des Saules, 18th arrondissement) or Le Sergent Recruteur (41 rue Saint-Louis-en-Ile, 4th arrondissement) may just salvage your trip to the Sacre Coeur or Notre Dame.

∽ THE ARRIVAL OF LOCALLY ROASTED COFFEE IN PARIS ∽

Parisians love spending endless hours at cafés, but the actual coffee served in many of these cafés leaves little reason to linger. Even in some of the city's most respected eating establishments, including an estimated 30 percent of Michelin-starred restaurants, the bang of a gastronomic meal ends with a whimper—in the form of a bitter, listless cup of coffee that came from a prepackaged pod.

Luckily, a growing group of energetic coffee advocates are providing an alternative for Parisians. Locally roasted, ethically sourced coffee is now available in coffee shops across the city—many of which are also developing workshop spaces and offering classes to consumers who want to understand how to make a truly great cup of coffee. In the span of just a few years, baristas and coffee roasters have taken on the challenge of bringing craft coffee to the city, with great success and appreciation.

When Coutume Café (47 rue de Babylone, 7th arrondissement) opened in 2011 it was one of the first in a new wave of Paris coffee shops that sourced and roasted their own beans. Their first location quickly found a following, drawn to the superlative lattes and exciting brunch and lunch options. Since opening their flagship shop, Coutume has unveiled a space that serves as a roasting workshop and tasting room (8 rue Martel, 10th arrondissement) as well as a Tokyo branch for Japanese francophile coffee lovers!

At about the same time, Café Lomi (3ter rue Marcadet, 18th arrondissement) was transitioning from being a wholesale roaster and supplier to adding its own coffee shop. They took over a high-ceilinged space in the Goutte d'Or neighborhood of Paris, an area where tourists often feared to tread. These new coffee-roasting neighbors quickly became an institution in the *quartier*, with their cozy couch, friendly service, and filter coffees becoming a winning combo for visitors from near and far. True to the spirit of the 18th arrondissement, community building and cultural exchange were quick to

follow. A prime example of neighborhood collaborations is the 3ter beer. Made with three types of coffee, three hops and malt varieties, and produced using a triple fermentation, the 3ter beer is the product of a partnership with the *Brasserie de la Goutte d'Or* (page 174). Café Lomi's spirit of adventure and curiosity is infectious and passed on to all who sip coffee there. Innovators in their field, the Lomi team came up with a novel way of explaining the flavor nuances of café to the terroir-minded French consumer by creating the Bordeaux and Bourgogne blends. These blends, with the Bordeaux being fuller and fruitier and the Bourgogne resembling its more acidic wine counterpart, speak a language the French can understand, and represent an inventive way of inviting novice coffee tasters to enjoy the experience.

More adventurous visitors are invited to explore interesting coffee pairings (espresso and bleu cheese!) and learn more about the process of coffee roasting in the workshop space in the back of the café. Facing the graffiti wall that this neighborhood was once best known for, Café Lomi has become a welcome addition to this diverse neighborhood.

In the neighboring 19th arrondissement, Belleville Brulerie (10 rue Pradier, 19th arrondissement) offers six unique coffee blends that are roasted on-site. Their Saturday cuppings (20 euro/person) now rival wine tastings (page 135) as the Parisians' favorite weekend pastime. If you can't make it to Belleville Brulerie, you can still enjoy their coffees in one of the many restaurants and cafés that source their beans, including *Holybelly* (page 79), Fondation (16 rue Dupetit Thouars, 3rd arrondissement), KB Café (53 ave Trudaine, 9th arrondissement), and as of late, in cafés as far as Bordeaux and Berlin!

The latest addition to the locally roasted coffee scene in Paris is L'Arbre à Café. Making its home on arguably the most gastronomic street in the city, the *rue du Nil* (page 72), L'Arbre à Café (10 rue du Nil, 2nd arrondissement) has a huge selection of carefully curated coffees all roasted in-house. Founder Hippolyte Courty has positioned his roastery as the distinguished product that it is, and you will often find the L'Arbre à Café team present not only at coffee events, but also wine tastings (such as the prestigious annual natural wine event La Dive Bouteille).

WINTER RECIPES

APPETIZERS, SIDES, SALADS, AND SOUPS

MARDI'S SUNCHOKE SOUP / *SOUPE DE TOPINAMBOUR*

This soup is a specialty of *Café Lumi* (page 84) chef Mardi Hartzog. A favorite menu item on a winter day at the café, this is also an easy soup to prepare at home. I use sunchokes from Marc Mascetti's stand at *Marché Monge* (page 167), but you can find these seasonal delights at almost any farmers' market in winter.

Mardi Hartzog and a fresh batch of Sunchoke Soup.

Ingredients

Serves 4

2 tablespoons butter

1 medium onion, chopped

1 clove garlic, diced

2 pounds (1 kilo) sunchokes, peeled and chopped (quickly blanching sunchokes before peeling them makes the skin much easier to remove)

6 cups (1½ liters) vegetable stock*

Salt and pepper

Preparation

In a medium-sized pot over medium heat, melt butter and sauté onion and garlic until barely translucent, about 5 minutes. Add sunchokes and vegetable stock. Let simmer about 30–40 minutes or until sunchokes are soft when you poke them with a fork. Blend together with an immersion blender until smooth. Make sure that the texture isn't too liquidy. If unsure if it is too liquidy, set aside some of the stock before blending, which can be added later. Add salt and pepper to taste and serve immediately.

For the vegetable stock:

Ingredients

1 tablespoon extra virgin olive oil
1 yellow onion, peeled and halved
1 medium carrot, washed and
   halved
1 stalk celery, peeled and halved
½ leek, coarsely chopped
9 cups (2 liters) water
2 teaspoons fine sea salt
1 teaspoon black pepper

Preparation

Heat olive oil in a large stock pot. Sauté onion until translucent; add other vegetables, and sauté until they are sweating and cooked, 8–10 minutes. Add water and bring to a boil. Add salt and pepper and cook on medium heat for another 5–10 minutes, until broth has taken on the flavor of the vegetables. Strain and set liquid aside to use in soup.

LA CUCINA DI TERRESA'S WINTER SQUASH ALMOND MILK SOUP

This hearty soup, which she calls "mightily savory," is one of Terresa Murphy's favorite winter meals. One batch can feed up to 8–10 people, making this a great option for dinner parties where all are invited to share the simple joys of plant-based cooking.

Ingredients

Serves 8–10

Zest of lime

2½ pounds (1.25 kilos) mixed winter squash; sweet dumpling, kabocha, butternut, blue Hubbard, etc.

4 tablespoons unsalted butter or extra virgin olive oil

Generous handful of pumpkin seeds, roasted and finely chopped

1 cup (100 grams) almonds

4¼ cups (1 liter) water

Unrefined sea salt

Freshly ground pepper (white, if you have it)

Preparation

Wash, dry, and zest lime, then set aside on a plate to slightly dry. Preheat the oven to 400°F (200°C). Scrub and dry the outside of squash. Cut in half and scoop out the seeds and filaments (don't throw away—cook up into a broth to sip on). Lightly brush the skin of each half with olive oil. Bake in a baking dish, cut side down, on the middle rack of the oven until easily pierced with a knife, 30–45 minutes, depending on size.

Let the oven cool to 325°F (160°C). Spread the pumpkin seeds out in a baking dish and toast in the oven on the middle rack for 10 minutes, or until they just begin to pop. Let cool and coarsely chop.

Either soak almonds for 24 hours prior to making the soup, changing water 2–3 times (no need to remove the skins in this case), or just before making the soup add dry almonds to a saucepan where generous amounts of water are boiling. When the water returns to a boil, cook for 1 minute. Strain and squeeze off the skins while almonds are still hot. Transfer the almonds to a blender jar or simply use an immersion blender. If using a blender, start off with just enough water to cover the almonds and blend at low speed until they are completely broken up. Gradually add the remaining water and blend at high speed until smooth and milky, about 1 minute. If using an immersion blender, put the almonds in a large, tall jar. Add half the amount of water and blend until smooth and silky. Add the remaining water and give a whir (this might need to be done in two batches). Place a nut milk bag over a good-sized pan, or drape a thin linen (or muslin) towel over it, and pour in the almond liquid. Begin twisting the bag (or linen, gathering up the ends and edges) tighter and tighter, pressing on the ball of the meal that forms while twisting, until all the almond milk has been extracted. Don't discard the almond meal; it can be used for plenty of things, like an addition to granola in the morning!

Cut each half of the roasted squash in large pieces. Add two or three to the almond milk in the pan and blend with an immersion blender until smooth. Add more of the squash bit by bit and blend until your soup has a nice creamy consistency, not too thick, not too thin (this can be done in a blender). Season with sea salt to taste.

Just before serving add the butter (or olive oil) to the soup and heat to just below boiling—do not let it boil—stirring occasionally. Check seasoning and add a bit of salt if needed. Ladle soup into bowls. Garnish with the lime zest and pumpkin seeds. Give a couple of good twists of freshly ground pepper.

CRUSHED WINTER SQUASH / ÉCRASÉ *DE POTIRON*

This recipe is inspired by the beautiful kabocha squash found in winter at Jean-Luc Dormoy's stand at *Marché Daumesnil* (page 59). Mme. Dormoy suggested they use the squash to prepare this simple *écrasé*, which is similar to a purée, but with hearty chunks of squash allowed to remain. You can use any kind of winter squash that has a dense flesh, but the kabocha squash and its striking bright orange flesh make for a lovely side dish for a winter dinner.

Ingredients

Serves 4

2 medium kabocha squash (if kabocha squash is not available, another variety, like acorn or butternut, will do), halved with seeds removed

¾ cup (180 grams) crème fraîche

Salt and pepper to taste

Preparation

After removing seeds from the squash, cut it into halves and then quarters.

Add squash to a pot and fill with enough water to just cover. Bring to a boil and let cook for 20–25 minutes, until tender. Remove from water (keep the water to the side in case it is needed later). Let squash cool 3–5 minutes, then remove the skin; it should peel off easily after being cooked.

Mash the flesh of the squash with a fork, adding the crème fraîche while mashing. The écrasé should be meaty and thick, just roughly mashed with some chunks remaining. Add spoonfuls of the water if more liquid is needed. Season with salt and pepper and serve immediately.

DEVILED EGGS WITH HOMEMADE MAYONNAISE / OEUFS MAYONNAISE

This is another recipe inspired by *La Pointe du Grouin* (page 79). Their hard-boiled eggs with homemade mayonnaise are a menu staple and a great start to a meal of small plates and sandwiches, paired with a carafe of natural wine, of course.

Ingredients

Serves 4

4 large eggs, hard-boiled (see below)

For the mayonnaise:

1 egg yolk, at room temperature
1 teaspoon Dijon mustard
1 pinch fine sea salt
½ cup (120 mL) extra virgin olive oil
4 tablespoons fresh parsley, coarsely chopped

Preparation

Place eggs in a medium-sized saucepan and cover with cold water. Slowly bring water to a boil. Cook for 10-12 minutes then immediately strain the eggs and place in a bowl of cold water to cool. Let eggs cool for 10–15 minutes. While waiting for eggs to cool, prepare the mayonnaise. In a small bowl, whisk together egg yolk, mustard, and salt until mixture becomes slightly creamy and light yellow in color, about 2–3 minutes. Slowly add olive oil in a thin stream while continuing to whisk. Consistency should remain creamy, and color should lighten as oil is whisked in. Continue adding oil, making sure the mayonnaise remains thick—all the olive oil may not be needed.

Remove eggs from cold water. Tap each egg lightly against a hard surface to break the shell, then slowly roll the egg against the hard surface to further break down the shell. Remove shell and cut the eggs in half. Arrange eggs, yolk side up, on four individual plates. Use a piping bag or a spoon to top each egg half with fresh mayonnaise. Sprinkle with chopped fresh parsley and serve immediately.

SHELL BEANS DRESSED IN OLIVE OIL WITH FRESH THYME / *SALADE DE HARICOTS À ECOSSER*

Fresh shell beans abound in autumn and winter months, making an ideal side dish for rich one-pot meals such as *Slow Cooked Chicken in Wine and Mushroom Sauce* (page 106). The first time I bought fresh shell beans in Paris was at *Marché Cours de Vincennes* (page 123), where Mme. Dormoy told me how to prepare the shucked beans as she scooped handfuls of them into a bag. Like all my favorite French recipes, this one was easy and ingredient-focused. A basic bouquet garni and some quality olive oil is all you need to accompany the buttery flavor of these humble yet savory beans.

Ingredients

Serves 6

4 cups (750 grams) shelled beans
1 dried bay leaf
2 garlic cloves, whole
4–5 sprigs of fresh or dried thyme
2 tablespoons extra virgin olive oil
Salt and pepper

Preparation

Place shelled beans in a large pot and cover with water. Add a bay leaf, garlic cloves, thyme, 1 tablespoon olive oil, salt, and pepper. Bring water to a boil and then lower to medium heat and cook 45–60 minutes, until beans are soft and cooked all the way through. Add water as necessary. Once cooked, drain off excess water from the beans and toss in remaining olive oil. Add salt and pepper to taste and serve warm.

OYSTERS WITH MIGNONETTE SAUCE /
HUITRES À LA SAUCE MIGNONETTE

Shucking oysters may seem like a daunting task best reserved for professionals and the very steady-handed, but after almost a decade of living in Paris, I decided it was time to have a go at it. As oysters are a staple at holiday meals and any table commemorating a special occasion, I started shucking a few each year, normally at Christmastime, getting steadily better at the delicate art of opening up these fickle bivalves. It wasn't until I spent two weeks doing the grape harvest in the Loire (page 12) that I perfected my technique, opening up almost sixty rocky oysters from Brittany for a team of hungry harvesters. The process of oyster shucking should not be taken lightly, as it is all too easy to pierce yourself with the oyster shucker as you snap open the slippery shellfish. Watch a few videos or have a seasoned pro show you the steps before you dive in.

Allow for at least six oysters per person and pay attention to the smell of the oysters as you open them; any with foul-smelling shells should be immediately discarded to avoid the infamous encounter with the symptoms of eating a bad oyster.

Ingredients

Serves 4
24 oysters

For the sauce:
4 tablespoons shallots, finely
    chopped
Two turns freshly ground black
    pepper
Salt
1 cup (240 mL) red wine vinegar

Preparation

Make your sauce in advance; it will be better the longer it is allowed to sit and infuse in the refrigerator. Stir shallots, pepper, and a dash of salt into your red wine vinegar. Cover and refrigerate at least 4 hours before serving.

Before shucking oysters, protect your oyster-holding hand with a clean dish towel that has been folded to provide a shield between the oyster shucker and your palm. You can also keep the back

of your hand against a hard surface, such as a countertop, to give more resistance as you shuck the oysters. Insert the point of the shucker into the seam of the oyster. It can be hard to find a point of entry and you may have to try a few different spots before you gain entry. Once you've gotten into the oyster, push forward to disconnect the muscle from the shell; you will feel a click and release once you've done that and you should be able to pry open the shell easily. Once open, pour out the juice (the oyster will quickly make fresh juice) and then replace the top shell. Serve on ice if eating later or on a large plate for immediate consumption. Remove mignonette sauce at the last minute and serve with a small spoon so people can eat it with their fresh oysters.

FRENCH ONION SOUP /
SOUPE À L'OIGNON GRATINÉE

This easy soup takes a little time, but that's what makes it so savory and filling. A bistrot favorite and a winter staple, this soup makes a perfect starter for a dinner party or a simple lunch amongst friends.

Ingredients

2 tablespoons (30 grams) salted butter
3 cups (350 grams) yellow onions, finely sliced
2 tablespoons all-purpose flour
½ cup (120 mL) dry white wine
3–5 fresh or dried thyme sprigs
1 dried bay leaf
Salt and pepper
8 cups (2 liters) beef stock
1 baguette, cut into ½ inch (2 cm) slices
2 cups (250 grams) grated Gruyère

Preparation

Melt butter on medium-high heat in a large pot. Add finely sliced onions and brown them, being careful not to let them burn (you can add water if necessary to prevent them from sticking to the pan). When onions are browned, after approximately 15–20 minutes, stir in flour followed by wine. Add thyme, bay leaf, and a dash of salt and pepper. Add beef stock and bring to a boil. Reduce heat to low and cover, cooking for 25–30 minutes, until soup slightly thickens.

Set oven to broil on high. In separate, oven-safe bowls, or in a large oven-safe pot, prepare the *gratin* portion of the soup. Place half the baguette slices, covered with half the cheese, on the bottom of the pot, or equal parts of half of the cheese and bread in four separate bowls already filled with soup. Place bowls or pot in the oven under high heat and let grill until cheese is melted and bread is slightly toasted. Top with a turn of ground pepper and serve immediately.

CRISP ENDIVE SALAD WITH ROQUEFORT SALAD AND WALNUTS / SALADE D'ENDIVES AU ROQUEFORT ET AUX NOIX

This recipe is inspired by my first experience living abroad in France. As an assistant language teacher in a rural high school in the small town of Mayenne, I had to adapt to a lot of cultural and lifestyle changes, one of which was figuring out what to do with local produce during the winter months. My local market had no shortage of endives, a vegetable that I hadn't eaten much of before moving to France. This simple salad, which combines one of my favorite French cheeses, Roquefort, and seasonal walnuts, became a favorite and a regular weeknight meal in my little town.

Ingredients

4–5 medium endives, cut into ½ inch (1 cm) slices
1 cup (120 grams) walnuts, roughly chopped
1 cup (120 grams) crumbled Roquefort
Dijon Vinaigrette (page 150)
Fresh ground pepper

Preparation

Wash endives, removing outer leaves if they are thin and wilting. Let dry and then cut into ½ inch (1 cm) slices. In a large salad bowl combine endives, chopped walnuts, and crumbled Roquefort. Toss with Dijon vinaigrette then finish with a turn of fresh ground pepper. Serve immediately, topped with remaining crumbled Roquefort.

SAUCE

BÉCHAMEL

This is the most basic of French sauces and the base of so many classic French recipes. It may seem intimidating at first, but once you get the hang of turning four simple ingredients into a luscious sauce you'll be whipping it up all the time. Don't be afraid to adjust as needed in order to get the desired consistency. The most important thing is having a smooth

sauce that is free of lumps. In order to do so, be sure the flour is well combined before adding milk. You can increase this recipe as needed; just make sure that you have equal parts butter and flour and add additional milk until you reach desired consistency.

Ingredients

⅔ cup (50 grams) butter
⅔ cup (50 grams) flour
2 cups (480 mL) skim milk
    (room temperature)
Dash nutmeg
Fine sea salt
Freshly ground black pepper

Preparation

Melt butter on medium heat in a saucepan. Once melted, begin to slowly whisk in flour until it becomes fully incorporated with butter, resulting in a uniform golden thickened consistency. Slowly add room temperature milk, whisking while pouring an even stream of the milk into the saucepan. Whisk until all the milk has been added, then bring to a low bubble and continue to stir until sauce is thick enough to stick to your spoon or spatula. Stir in a dash of nutmeg and season with salt and pepper to taste.

MAINS

HOLYBELLY'S BEEF CHEEK STEW WITH FRIED POLENTA AND SALAD / RAGOÛT DE JOUE DE BOEUF À L'ANCIENNE, POLENTA CROUSTILLANTE, SALADE DE PETITES FEUILLES

This hearty recipe was featured on Holybelly chefs Sarah Mouchot and Lise Kvan's winter 2014 menu. Marinating the beef cheek in wine and seasonings overnight, or for several hours, brings out the delicate flavors of this often-overlooked cut of meat. Fresh seasonal carrots and turnips complement this perfect meal for a cold winter day.

Sarah had these thoughts to share on her recipe: "This beef cheek ragoût is rich, delicious and a 'cheek'y homage to my dad's cooking, who, like a good Frenchman, likes to cook things very low and slow with a lot of red wine!

"At Holybelly we like to cook the food that makes us happy and reminisce on the dishes of our childhood. But we also have other goals: generating as little waste as possible, respecting our produce's origin, and creating dishes that are both delicious and good for you. I like to call this 'honest cooking.' This ragoût, made with cheek, is the best for this. Cheek is not a very popular part of the animal and it is such a good feeling to get a tough cut of meat and turn it into melt-in-your-mouth deliciousness! Also, although cheek is considered as offal, it is actually a muscle, which should be considered as a piece of meat. It is a very lean piece at that, since cows spend their entire day chewing grass!

"This ragoût is also a very good way to get rid of your red wine leftovers. I usually pour all of my 'fonds de bouteille' into one bottle, and when I get a full bottle, it's time to get cooking!

"The only secret to this recipe? Time. Cooking time of course (the longer, the better), but also, making this ragoût a day before serving it makes it even more tender and complex. Trust me, it is worth it."

Ingredients

Serves 4

1 large white onion, diced
3 garlic cloves, sliced
4 branches of fresh or dried thyme
2 sprigs of fresh or dried rosemary
2 dried bay leaves
1¾ pound (800 grams) beef cheek
2 medium carrots, diced
1 medium turnip or parsnip or beetroot, diced
1 bottle full-bodied red wine (Cotes du Rhone works well)
Salt
Pepper
Vegetable oil
6 tablespoons (100 grams) tomato paste

Preparation

Tip from the chef (this step is optional, but will give the dish even more depth): The day before cooking the ragoût (preferably two days before you actually plan on eating it!), place the onion, garlic, thyme, rosemary, and bay leaves into a bowl and cover with the beef cheeks. Add the carrots and other vegetables and pour the red wine. Lightly season with salt and pepper and mix in a bit. Cover and place in the fridge. The next day, strain the red wine marinade out of the meat and veggies.

In a pot (preferably cast iron), heat the cooking oil (medium heat) and brown the beef cheek. Remove the meat from the pot and place in a side dish. Re-oil the pan and add in the onion. Slowly sweat the onion and begin to caramelize it lightly. Once the onion starts to color, add in the carrots, turnip, parsnip or beetroot, and garlic. Continue to caramelize all the vegetables together, lightly and on medium-low heat.

Once the vegetables have cooked for about 15 minutes and begin to soften, add in the tomato paste. Cook the tomato paste and vegetables for about 5 minutes, stirring frequently to make sure it does not stick. Deglaze with the red wine and make sure to reincorporate any caramelization that might be at the bottom of the pan. Let cook to reduce wine, about 5 –7 minutes.

Add the beef cheeks back into the pot, pour in the stock or water so that everything is submerged in liquid, and give it a good stir. Cover the pot with a lid and slow cook on the stove for 3 to 4 hours on medium-low heat. The beef cheeks are cooked when they are completely tender and melt in your mouth. If not, give them another 30 minutes on the stove.

When the beef cheeks are cooked, turn off the heat and let the ragoût cool down in the liquid, at least 3 hours. Letting the ragoût cool down in the liquid before straining it makes for an even more tender meat.

Strain the cooking liquid from the pot into a smaller saucepan and reduce on high heat to create a jus de boeuf. The jus de boeuf is ready when it has thickened into a sauce and is glossy.

Once you've made your *Crispy Polenta Squares* (page 102), heat up the beef cheek ragoût in a saucepan, with a little jus de boeuf and some water if needed. Season to taste.

In another saucepan, heat up the jus de boeuf. Season to taste. When the ragoût is almost done, place the freshly fried polenta onto the plates. Top with the hot beef ragoût. Spoon over some jus de boeuf, and finish with a crisp salad garnish (page 103) on top to add freshness, crunchiness, and volume to the plate.

CRISPY POLENTA SQUARES

Ingredients

Serves 4

1½ cups (360 mL) heavy cream
1½ cups (360 mL) milk
1½ cups (360 mL) water
2 bay leaves
1 sprig fresh thyme
1 sprig fresh rosemary
1 garlic clove, crushed
Salt and pepper
1¾ cups (200 grams) quick
  cooking polenta (should cook
  in 2–3 minutes per package
  instructions)

Preparation

Line a square (8 in x 8 in, 20 cm x 20 cm) or rectangular baking dish with plastic wrap. In a saucepan, heat the cream, milk, and water with the herbs and crushed garlic. Season to taste with salt and pepper. Slowly bring to a simmer, then turn off heat, cover, and set aside to infuse for 15 minutes. Strain the liquid into a larger saucepan, bring back to a simmer, and whisk the polenta in over low heat. Whisk and cook until thickened, about 2 minutes.

Pour the polenta mix into the baking dish and flatten with an additional layer of plastic wrap on top. Place in the fridge to cool and harden, at least three hours. Once solidified, cut the polenta into squares (1 in x 1 in or 3 cm x 3 cm is a nice size, as it allows for nice crunch and a nice melty inside).

If you have a fryer, deep fry at 420°F, or 220°C, for about 3 minutes or until golden.

If you don't have a fryer, heat neutral cooking oil into a pan, place polenta squares in pan, and cook until golden; then, using a tong, turn each square and cook the other side.

Once cooked, toss the polenta squares in a bowl covered with paper towel, to get rid of excess oil.

GARNISH

Ingredients

Serves 4

1 cup (100 grams) watercress

2 small carrots, peeled and sliced
  or grated (purple or yellow
  carrots make for a fancier
  plating!)

Salt

Pepper

Dash apple cider vinegar

1 tablespoon extra virgin olive oil

Preparation

Wash watercress and lightly rip it into smaller, easy-to-serve portions. Take peeled carrots and, using a mandoline if you have one (otherwise, use a grater to grate carrots), slice the carrots lengthwise. Place carrot slices in ice-cold water so they curl.

In a bowl, mix the watercress and carrots and add salt, pepper, apple cider vinegar, and good quality olive oil to taste.

SAUERKRAUT / *CHOUCROUTE GARNIE*

In the early stages of my love affair with home fermentation projects, sauerkraut, or *choucroute*, became a staple of my diet. Inspired by Sandor Katz's wonderful book *Wild Fermentation*, I experimented with all kinds of variations on this simple fermented cabbage, which is full of healthy probiotics, giving a great boost to your immune system during the winter months.

The French enjoy their sauerkraut garnished with a selection of cured meats and boiled potatoes. You can ask your butcher for advice on quantities and varieties that will make good accompaniments.

Ingredients

Serves 6

For the sauerkraut (to be prepared at least a week in advance):

5 pounds (2 kilograms) Savoy cabbage, thinly sliced or grated

3 tablespoons coarse sea salt

2 tablespoons juniper berries or black peppercorns, or one of each

Optional: grated carrots, grated brussels sprouts, thinly sliced apples, sliced onions

For the garniture:

3 pounds (1.25 kilos) cured meat

12 small potatoes, peeled and boiled

Preparation

In a large crock or food-grade plastic bucket, layer thinly sliced or grated cabbage with pinches of sea salt and juniper berries and/or peppercorns. Alternate these three ingredients, creating levels of evenly distributed cabbage, salt, and seasonings. It is important that the salt is equally distributed among the cabbage, as this is instrumental in extracting liquid from the cabbage and creating the juice, or brine, that the mixture will ferment in. Other optional fruits and vegetable can be added, along with the cabbage, in the preparation of the sauerkraut. Punch ingredients down into the crock/bucket, ensuring that the mixture is compact and as airtight as possible. Cover the cabbage mixture with a plate or surface that fits just inside the top and then place a weight on this surface (a jar filled with water or dried beans or something equally heavy works well). The weight will push the sauerkraut and, in early stages, help to extract the liquid from the cabbage, and then eventually keep the cabbage submerged in the resulting brine.

Press down occasionally on this weight, every few hours if possible, to help extract the most liquid possible in the first 24 hours. After one day; there should be enough brine to cover the cabbage; at this point the sauerkraut will begin to ferment on its own. It may be necessary to press down on the weight if the mixture is not fully covered in brine during the fermentation process. Add additional salt to the mixture if not enough brine has been created. Taste the sauerkraut every few days; it will get tangier over time. When sauerkraut has reached desired taste, simply transfer it to an airtight container and store in the refrigerator for future use.

The French cook their sauerkraut in wine (usually an Alsatian Riesling) until it becomes soft, sometimes keeping it on low heat for up to 45 minutes. I find this method diminishes both the taste and health benefits of raw sauerkraut, so I will often either mildly heat up my sauerkraut or just leave it untouched.

Arrange each plate with a serving of sauerkraut accompanied by boiled potatoes and a selection of cured meats. Serve with a Riesling or other Alsatian white wine.

SLOW-COOKED CHICKEN IN WINE AND MUSHROOM SAUCE / *COQ AU VIN*

While expats often miss the family they've left behind, one of the advantages to living abroad is choosing a brand-new family made up of friends and fellow foreigners. My Paris family makes a point of coming together on a regular basis for family dinners, often around my dinner table. It can be a bit daunting to cook for large groups, but the more the merrier—and a simple coq au vin is one of my favorite dishes for feeding a big group of cherished friends and newfound family.

Ingredients

Serves 6

Vegetable oil

½ pound (150 grams) diced bacon

4 pounds (2 kilos) chicken; mixture of thighs, breasts, drumsticks, and wings

10 small white or yellow onions

2 garlic cloves, pressed

1 dried bay leaf

Freshly ground black pepper

1 teaspoon fine sea salt

¼ teaspoon dried thyme

3 tablespoons all-purpose flour

2 cups (480 mL) full-bodied red wine

2 cups (480 mL) beef or chicken stock

2 tablespoons tomato paste

2 cups (300 grams) button mushrooms, sliced

Preparation

Heat oil on medium heat in a large pot* and cook bacon until it renders its fat. In the meantime, wash the chicken and then dry pieces with a clean dish towel. After about 5 minutes, remove bacon, leaving the rendered fat in the pot, and set aside. Add more oil if necessary, and arrange chicken pieces in one layer on the bottom of the pot. Cook while turning the chicken occasionally for 6–8 minutes. If you are browning your chicken in two separate pots, you can combine the meat in the larger of the two after it has been browned. Add onions, garlic, bay leaf, pepper, salt, and thyme. Cover and cook on low heat for 5–8 minutes. Add flour, lightly coating the chicken. Add red wine and stock, stirring to make sure there are no clumps of flour in your sauce. Add the cooked bacon and tomato paste. Cover and cook for 20 minutes, or until meat is tender. The chicken should be easily pierced with a fork. If this is not the case, continue cooking until flesh can easily be removed from the bone. Add mushrooms, cover, and cook an additional 3–5 minutes, or until mushrooms are done. At this point you can taste your sauce and season as necessary. If the sauce is not thick enough, bring the pot to a quick boil until desired consistency is reached. Serve with rice or *Shell Beans Dressed in Olive Oil with Fresh Thyme* (page 94).

*It is important not to crowd the chicken, so if you have more chicken than room in your pot, you can use two different pots for the browning step.

RAINY DAY CHEESE SOUFFLÉ / SOUFFLÉ AU FROMAGE

This dish never fails to elicit *oohs* and *ahhs* from dinner guests. A great way to brighten up a rainy day, this soufflé can be made quite quickly and should be watched attentively in order to get the perfect golden finish in the oven.

Ingredients

Serves 4
Béchamel Sauce (page 99)
4 medium-sized eggs, separated
3 cups (120 grams) grated
   Gruyère cheese
Fine sea salt
Freshly ground black pepper

Preparation

Preheat oven to 375°F (190°C). Butter a soufflé dish. In a small saucepan on medium heat, prepare a béchamel sauce. Once sauce has thickened, stir egg yolks in one by one, until fully combined. Add cheese in small handfuls and stir until fully melted. Add a dash of salt and pepper. Remove sauce from heat. In a separate bowl, beat egg whites until they form peaks. Pour béchamel and egg yolk mixture into buttered soufflé pan. Incorporate egg whites by folding them into the soufflé pan in small batches. Once all egg whites have been incorporated, place soufflé pan in oven and bake 20–25 minutes, until it has risen and a toothpick comes out clean—the soufflé should be golden and baked on top, but still wiggle when shaken. Serve immediately.

DESSERTS

MONT SALÈVE CHOCOLATE IMPERIAL STOUT CAKE / GÂTEAU STOUT DU MONT SALÈVE

Making this cake is similar to preparing one of my favorite Julia Child recipes for her famous *Reine de Saba* (page 115). This equally gourmand stout cake uses locally brewed stout, a modification I think that Julia would be a fan of.

Many French brewers make their own stout varieties, but the rich notes of La Brasserie du Mont Salève's Tzarine Imperial Stout are a perfect fit for this cake. Located in the Haut-Savoie region, close to Geneva, the Brasserie du Mont Salève is known for its wide range of impressive beers, which have been featured on the menus of some of the most acclaimed gastronomic destinations in nearby Lyon.

I buy bottles of Mont Salève brews at one of my favorite beer shops, *A la Bière Comme à la Bière* (page 177), but if you can't get your hands on this particular bottle, you will be fine using any dry and fairly bitter stout or porter with an alcohol content of at least 8 percent.

You can use the *glaçage* used for the Queen of Sheba Cake to ice this loaf cake, or leave it without icing, whichever you prefer.

Ingredients

¼ cup (85 grams / 3 ounces) semisweet chocolate squares

¼ cup (60 mL) freshly brewed, strong coffee

1½ cups (185 grams) flour

2 teaspoons baking powder

½ teaspoon baking soda

Preparation

Preheat oven to 375°F (190°C). Butter and flour a 12-inch (30 cm) rectangular loaf tin and set aside. Melt chocolate into coffee in a small saucepan over medium heat, until fully melted. Set aside to cool. Whisk together flour, baking powder, baking soda, and salt. In a separate bowl, cream together butter and 1 cup (200 grams) sugar. Add egg yolks one by

1 teaspoon salt
1 stick (110 grams) softened
   butter
1 cup (200 grams) + 3
   tablespoons sugar
2 medium-sized eggs, separated
½ cup (120 mL) stout or porter

one. Stir in cooled chocolate mixture followed by the stout or porter. Stir in flour mixture in batches. In a separate bowl, beat egg whites until they begin to thicken. Add 3 tablespoons of sugar and continue to beat until you get medium peaks. Slowly fold into batter. Stir in half of the egg whites and then in separate batches carefully fold remaining egg whites into the batter. Pour batter into the cake pan and tap against a hard surface to settle. Bake for 50–60 minutes, or until a toothpick comes out clean. Let cool in pan 15 minutes, remove, and cool on a cooling rack for at least 1 hour before serving.

KING'S CAKE WITH ALMOND PASTE / GALETTE DES ROIS

Nothing says January in Paris like a Galette des Rois after the busy holiday season winds down. This flaky, almond cream filled cake shows up in bakery windows across the city, extending the holiday cheer and bringing people together for King's Cake parties that extend the festivity of the otherwise frosty months.

After many attempts, this recipe was finally perfected with the help of baking guru Melanie Vaz, founder of *Gâteaux Mama*. The trick is to make sure your pastry is well-sealed after being filled with decadent *crème d'amande*. You can use store-bought puff pastry, or if you're feeling adventurous follow the recipe to make your own. Either way, be sure to fold and pinch the top and bottom layers of your galette to avoid leakage!

The *fève*, or prize, that is hidden in the cake was originally a bean and is now more commonly a porcelain miniature, often of iconic French figures or objects. If you happen to be traveling in France, check out flea markets or *brocantes* to find inexpensive vintage fèves to use in your gâteau; otherwise, keep with tradition and stow a dried bean away in your galette before baking. The ritual for cutting and serving the Galette des Rois holds that the youngest member of the group hides under the table as the host cuts pieces, waiting for the hidden child to call out names and decide who should be served each slice. The finder of the fève becomes King or Queen for the day and can choose a partner to help reign over their ephemeral kingdom.

Ingredients

17 ounces (500 grams) *Puff Pastry* (page 114)

Preparation

Prepare the crème d'amande filling by beating softened butter until creamy. In a separate bowl, whisk together sugar, almond flour, cornstarch,

For the filling:
8 tablespoons (125 grams)
    softened unsalted butter
¾ cup (130 grams) unrefined
    sugar
1½ cups (145 grams) almond flour
1 tablespoon cornstarch
1 pinch fine sea salt
1 tablespoon Grand Marnier
    (rum would also work)
2 large eggs

For the egg wash:
1 egg yolk
1 tablespoon water

Don't forget:
1 porcelain figurine or a dried
    bean
1 or 2 crowns for the Queen(s)
    and/or King(s)

and salt. Add the creamed butter and use hands to combine mixture until smooth. Stir in alcohol and then add eggs, one at a time. When eggs are fully combined, cover bowl with plastic wrap and keep in the refrigerator for at least an hour or as long as overnight.

Preheat oven to 360°F (180°C). Remove puff pastry dough from refrigerator and knead out onto a floured surface. Form dough into a smooth rectangle, then use a rolling pin to roll the dough out, being careful to not push too hard or overwork the pastry, until it is about three times its original size. Be gentle when rolling and maintain streaks of butter; the dough should be slightly marbled.

Fold both ends of the rectangular dough to meet in the middle, then turn the dough 90° to the right and roll it out once again until it is three times its size. Repeat folding and rolling out twice more, keeping gentle pressure with the rolling pin. On the final roll out, fold dough ends to meet each other and then cover with plastic wrap and refrigerate for 20 minutes to an hour before rolling out to use for the cake.

If using store-bought puff pastry, remove from packaging and roll out on a flat surface.

Use a plate or other circular stencil that is no larger than 12 inches (30 cm) in diameter. Use a knife to trace around the round object, making two circles of pastry, one being slightly larger (by about ¼ inch, or 6 mm) than the other.

Place the smaller of the two pastry circles on a piece of parchment paper. In a small bowl, whisk egg yolk with water until smooth. Use a pastry brush to generously coat the outer rim (a width of about 1 inch or 2½ cm) with the egg wash.

Using a spatula, evenly spread the crème d'amande filling in the center of the larger pastry circle. Once all the filling has been spread out, place the fève of your choice in the filling, not too far from the edge of the pastry dough (save some egg wash to use on the top of the cake before baking). Top the cake with the second pastry round, smoothing it over the crème d'amande; fold the edge of the larger pastry circle under the edge of the bottom layer, and then firmly press pastry together to seal the cake.

Decorate the top of the galette using the tip of a sharp knife. Create a classic chevron design or other pattern that will cover the cake top. When finished decorating, brush the top of the galette with remaining egg wash. With a sharp knife, poke five holes into the top of the cake, one in the center and four around the edges of the galette. Transfer galette, with parchment paper, to a rimmed baking sheet and place on middle rack of the oven and bake for 30–35 minutes, until puffy and golden brown.

Remove from oven and let cool to room temperature before serving.

PUFF PASTRY

Ingredients

2 cups (240 grams) all-purpose
   flour
1 teaspoon fine sea salt
1 cup (225 grams) unsalted
   butter, at room temperature
½ cup (120 mL) cold water

Preparation

Sift flour into a medium mixing bowl, and stir in
salt. Break butter into medium-sized chunks and
combine them into flour and salt mixture by
massaging them in with clean hands. Combine
until mixture sticks together and can form a loose
ball incorporating most of the flour, with some
chunks of butter remaining.

Make a well in the butter and flour mixture and
slowly add the cold water. Stir together until dough
becomes firm, adding remaining water as needed.
Form dough into a ball and cover bowl with plastic
wrap, then place it in the refrigerator for at least 20
minutes or as long as overnight.

QUEEN OF SHEBA CAKE / LA REINE DE SABA

Julia Child famously said "A party without a cake is just a meeting." I love to make this classic Julia recipe for our monthly Paris Ladies Collective meetings, when a group of passionate female expat entrepreneurs come together to talk about their projects, but also enjoy a moment of exchange and amusement *ensemble*. Whether you're going to a meeting or a party, this rich, nutty cake will be appreciated by all.

Ingredients

1 cup (160 grams) almonds, blanched and finely ground

⅔ cup (140 grams) + 2 tablespoons unrefined sugar

⅔ cup (115 grams/4 ounces) semisweet chocolate

3 tablespoons strong freshly brewed coffee

¼ pound (1 stick/115 grams) softened salted butter

3 medium-sized eggs, separated

⅓ cup (40 grams) sifted all-purpose flour

For the icing:

⅓ cup (60 grams) semisweet chocolate

3 tablespoons strong freshly brewed coffee

6 tablespoons (85 grams) softened salted butter

Preparation

Preheat oven to 375°F (190°C). Butter and flour an 8-inch (20 cm) round cake pan. Blanche almonds by boiling them in a large pot of water for 30–60 seconds. Remove almonds with a slotted spoon and keep the pot of water boiling as you take off the almond skins. Once this is completed, place the almonds in a blender with 1 tablespoon sugar. Blend until finely ground and set aside. Melt chocolate and coffee over the pot of boiling water. Stir until smooth and fully melted, then set aside to cool. In a large mixing bowl, cream together the stick of butter and ⅔ cup sugar. Beat egg yolks into sugar and butter mixture one by one, until fully combined. Stir cooled chocolate into butter mixture, then add ground almonds. In a small mixing bowl, use clean, dry beaters to beat egg whites until they form peaks. Add 1 tablespoon of sugar and continue beating until firm peaks form (the egg whites should stick to an overturned spatula). Set aside. Stir in ¼ of beaten egg whites. Add sifted flour. Fold in egg whites in batches until combined. Transfer batter to cake pan. Spread batter with a spatula to evenly distribute and tap lightly against a countertop or hard surface to remove air bubbles. Bake 20–25 minutes, until cake has risen, but is slightly shaky in the middle. Once baked, let cool in cake pan for 15 minutes. Remove from pan and let cool for an additional 30 minutes before icing.

To make the icing, melt together chocolate and coffee in a saucepan over a pot of boiling water. Once melted, remove from heat and stir in butter, one tablespoon at a time. Set saucepan in a bowl of ice-cold water and continue to stir until the mixture cools to a thick, spreadable consistency. Use a spatula to spread over cooled cake. Use additional almonds to decorate as you wish, using either whole almonds or chopped almonds to sprinkle over the top of the cake.

SPRING

Spring hits Paris in fits and starts, with the ever-changing weather patterns bringing constant surprises to the city's sky. The early riser will have a refreshing view of springtime Paris, accompanied by the crisp air and excitement that comes with the promise of warmer weather to come. Market stands are set up on freshly cleaned sidewalks and terraces as gutters gush streams of water that wash away the previous evening's revelry. Asparagus, turnips, cucumbers, and baby greens appear in markets and on restaurant menus while glasses of rosé are sipped outdoors at neighboring bistrots and cafés. This season is a great time for food shopping in Paris, as markets fill up with fair-weather vendors and shoppers, giving an extra burst of life to the market scene.

The unofficial start of spring in France is May 1st, or the *Fête du Travail*, a national holiday which is celebrated in part by purchasing bouquets of lily of the valley. Freelance florists from rural areas surrounding Paris come to the city to sell freshly harvested bunches of the delicate lilies, or *muguets*. Along with lilacs, these flowers have come to symbolize the arrival of spring in France. Throughout the month of May you will see flower vendors sprout up on street corners and in front of cafés. Markets also take part in this annual event, adding flair to their stands with buckets of flowering branches and sweet-smelling sprouts.

In Season: *apples, artichokes, asparagus, carrots, cauliflower, cherries, cucumbers, leeks, onions, potatoes, radishes, rhubarbs, strawberries, turnips*

MARCHÉ BIOLOGIQUE DE BATIGNOLLES

BOULEVARD DE BATIGNOLLES, 75017
Mº PLACE DE CLICHY (LINE 13) OR ROME (LINE 2)
OPEN: SATURDAY, 9:00 A.M.–2:00 P.M.

One of three of Paris's *marchés biologiques*, or organic markets, Marché Biologique des Batignolles takes up a series of blocks in the 17th arrondissement. While the vendors here are all certified organic, not all are actual producers, so one must keep an eye out for farm-fresh produce. The farmers from Au Val du Coutant bring seasonal fruits and vegetables to the market from their farm in Chailly-en-Brie, located forty-one miles from Paris. The selection is concentrated to a few hardy seasonal varieties, due mostly to the fact that the farm does not grow with the aid of greenhouses.

The fresh fruits and vegetables are high quality and indicative of what is truly in season in the region. Patricia, the stand's friendly vendor, is happy to explain to visitors what is in season on the farm as well as give suggestions on how to prepare whatever lovely, fresh vegetables you decide to take home with you. Across from the Au Val du Coutant stand you'll find Hermione Boehrer, whose farm is in Coulommiers, forty miles outside of Paris. Hermione specializes in herbs, wheatgrass (which you can purchase in shot or juice form at her stand), baby greens, potted herbs and flowers, and organic potting soil. Her bright green sorrel leaves are ideal for *Sorrel Sauce* (page 155), which is traditionally served with fish. You can also visit Hermione and Patricia at *Marché Raspail* (page 165).

If you're looking for nonperishables to take home, keep an eye out for the bulk grains and dried fruits stand squeezed between a cheesemonger and a producer from Auvergne. Here you will find not only organic dried goods but also a selection of homemade chocolates. Ask the vendor to break off a slab of dark, milk, or white chocolate—all of which make for a great afternoon treat or gift.

Pick up a bottle of farm-fresh cider from Michel Beucher, who will serenade you with one of his original compositions if the mood strikes. Grown on their orchard in Normandy, Thérèse and Michel's apples and pears make amazing juices and alcohols that are typical of the region.

Don't leave the market without stopping for a *Potato Pancake* (page 144) at Les Galatin's stand. Grab one hot off the griddle and enjoy it as you tour the market—you may like them so much you'll be tempted to try to make them at home!

PROFILE: HERMIONE BOEHRER: QUEEN OF BABY GREENS

Hermione Boehrer refers to her small farm in Coulommiers as "La Domaine du Château...sans château!" While there may not be a castle on site, Hermione lives on the land she works, in a small home whose façade is hidden by rosebushes that begin to blossom and climb in the spring months.

Hermione works her land seven days a week and largely on her own. But she will be the first to attest that she has "many angels" among her helpers. One sunny day, Hermione hosted me on a visit of her 2 ½ acres of land. During our walk we stumbled upon one of these angels, a woman in her early sixties named Geneviève, a regular customer at Marché Raspail, where Hermione has a stand on Sundays. Geneviève came to Hermione's land to lend a hand picking berries on the farm. In exchange for her volunteer work, she planned to take some of her harvest home to make a *Countryside Clafouti* (page 193).

Berries such as black currants and raspberries are an anomaly among Hermione's harvest. The farmer's true specialty is the baby sprouts and shoots of aromatic herbs that make her market stand easy to spot from afar, with its overflowing bunches of fresh rosemary, thyme, and verbena. Such variety and selection of fresh herbs is rare at Paris markets, and shoppers come from near and far to stock up on their favorite herbs from Hermione's garden. Hermione has a strategic reason for creating her aromatic and agricultural niche. "We have to distinguish ourselves from the other vendors at the market if we want to be successful," Hermione explains. In the face of large-scale growers and imported vegetables at the markets, the industrious farmer decided to focus on the delicate world of herbs, young shoots, and varieties that grow easily in the region and throughout the year.

A new addition to Hermione's repertoire is kale, or *chou kale* as it has come to be known in French, which has quickly become popular amongst curious shoppers. "I sell it *à la négatif*!" Hermione says about her strategy for selling kale to the French. "I tell them, 'it's not very good—only the Americans buy it' and then all the French say, 'I want some!'" Hermione's sales approach works—but the true reason for her success at the market is the quality of her produce, grown with painstaking care and attention in Hermione's castle-free kingdom.

MARCHÉ COURS DE VINCENNES

COURS DE VINCENNES, 75012
M° PICPUS (LINE 6)
OPEN: WEDNESDAY AND SATURDAY, 7:00 A.M.–2:30 P.M.

The Marché Cours de Vincennes attracts locals and adventurous shoppers to this far-flung part of town, whose residential feel and traffic-filled thoroughfare make it an unlikely stop on a tourist's itinerary. Those who make the trip will be rewarded with a market that is truly a diamond in the rough due to its large selection of local farmers selling fruits and vegetables from the Île-de-France region.

Monsieur Martinet sells seasonal produce grown on his farm, located nineteen miles from Paris. Despite the increasing cost of land in the outskirts of Paris, Martinet has maintained his family farm rather than selling to developers. He brings homegrown goods to several markets on a weekly basis—an impressive feat, given that he does both the farming and marketing of his produce all on his own. In the spring you will find a wide range of seasonal vegetables at his stand, including green onions, baby turnips, carrots, and radishes, all perfect fixings for a *Parchment Baked Sea Bass with Spring Vegetables* (page 152). You can also buy vegetables from Mr. Martinet at *Marché Bastille* (page 15).

Further down the market you'll find Bernard Groult, whose farm is also in the Île-de-France, more specifically the Val d'Oise department less than an hour north of Paris. Groult's proximity to the city guarantees some of the freshest produce at the market, including mixed baby greens, conference pears, and bunches of aromatic lilacs to round out your spring shopping basket. While at the stand, pick up a half dozen rhubarb stalks to make a simple *Rhubarb Compote* (page 158).

The cheerful ladies at the Villedieu stand located at the western end of Marché Cours de Vincennes are the proud proprietors of some of the season's first locally grown strawberries. Get to the market early to grab a *barquette* before they sell out—they go fast!

PARIS COMMUNITY GARDENS

It's hard to find anything more local in Paris than vegetables, fruits, and flowers cultivated within city limits. Green-thumbed urbanites or those seeking solace from the city are able to find a haven thanks to a city-sponsored community garden charter called La Charte Main Verte. This charter supports the creation of shared gardens in Paris and has helped develop over eighty community gardens across the city in the past ten years.

Locating these hidden oases is not always easy, but a list of *jardins partagés* can be found on the city of Paris website, and more information is available through Jardinons Ensemble.

The 18th arrondissement, with its abandoned lots and railroad tracks, is home to numerous community gardens, including Les Jardins du Ruisseau, which is located on the border of Paris and the neighboring suburb of St. Ouen. The garden consists of a series of raised bed plots that occupy the deserted platforms of the *petite ceinture*, the inner ring of Paris's defunct commuter rail system. Les Jardins du Ruisseau offers residents, school groups, and visitors the opportunity to enjoy a bit of calm and greenery away from the city's commotion. In the springtime shared plots begin to overflow as rosebushes, grape vines, and raspberry bushes reclaim their space, and strawberries and

cherry tomatoes start to change from green to red, ready to be plucked by their attentive caretakers. The gardens are also home to beehives that produce award-winning honey and a chicken coop that boasts some of the city's most fabulous urban hens, who produce eggs for their lucky caretakers.

Gardens like Les Jardin du Ruisseau contribute significantly to the biodiversity of Paris, while offering an opportunity for the city's youngest residents to come in contact with nature. They also provide a habitat for the city's most unexpected residents, including threatened insect species and the elusive but endearing Parisian hedgehog.

If you can't make it to Les Jardins du Ruisseau, the *petite ceinture* railway can also be enjoyed through a series of walkways that transform the abandoned platforms into charming trails that take the wanderer on an urban safari. The newest stretch of the beltway to be open to the public is in the 15th arrondissement, between the Georges Brassens and André Citroën parks.

FORAGED HERBAL TEAS SOURCED FROM THE CITY

Foraging for fresh herbs and edible plants can seem impossible in a city like Paris, with its meticulously kept gardens and their fervently protected patches of grass. Despite the lack of wild, wide-open spaces in Paris, it is possible to glean some lovely ingredients if you know where to look. Paris-based herbalist Marilyn Brentegani has a list of spots around the city that are abundant in wild flowers, plants, and herbs. Marilyn leads plant identification tours of the Bois de Vincennes, a large forested park on the eastern edge of Paris, where you are introduced to the prolific flora of the prairies and canopies of the park.

Nettles, elderflower, linden, wild rose, and plantain are just a few vitamin-rich, healing plants that one can find while strolling through the woods with Marilyn, who often offers guided visits through Taste Tours. The Bois de Vincennes is not the only place one can find such treasures. Certain parks in Paris have been left to their own devices, creating perfect environments for wild plants to thrive. This was proven when Marilyn was kind enough to give me a tour of the Parc de Belleville in the 20th arrondissement, where I learned of the many edible plants that surround us in our everyday city lives.

After that tour, I started seeing herbal tea ingredients everywhere—in parks, in balcony gardens, and in my own community garden. Exploring the city with my new set of eyes, I discovered an abundance of herbal tea options, including rose petals, lavender, mint, rosemary, fennel, and raspberry leaves. It turns out the city is a great place to source your next cup of tea!

While foraging, it is important to remember not to upset the natural balance of an ecosystem. The bees might need that extra handful of lavender or linden more than you, so take only what you need. In France, especially in particularly forage-friendly areas around the country, pharmacists are trained in identifying wild plants, providing an invaluable resource that protects gleaners from ingesting potentially fatal finds. If you are unsure or unable to identify a plant you have picked, be sure to check with a reliable field guide or professional.

Drying roots and petals to conserve them for a longer time is simple and straightforward. Be sure to wash the plants before drying, as it is difficult to remove dirt afterward. You can either hang herbs from a string or set them aside on a clean dish towel and allow them to dry. If you decide you don't want to drink any of your foraged items, save them for your next soak—dried herbs and flowers are great bath time additions!

Here are some suggestions for herbal tea combinations, using herbs and plants that are fairly ubiquitous, even in urban areas. Marilyn advises using hot, not boiling, water when preparing a fresh herbal tea, especially when using fresh flowers (which are more fragile than dried flowers, leaves, or roots).

MINT AND NETTLE HERBAL TEA

Be sure to use young nettle leaves for this tea—they should be picked in early spring, before they flower. Choose the top leaves of a plant and handle them carefully so that you don't get stung; gloves are a good idea when foraging for nettles! The plant is rendered harmless after it's been blanched in boiling water for 30 seconds to a minute. After blanching the nettles, you can either dry them or use them immediately. Combined with either fresh or dried mint, this makes a refreshing spring tea.

Ingredients

1 cup (240 mL) hot (not boiling) water
1 tablespoon fresh or dried nettle leaves
1 tablespoon fresh or dried mint leaves

Preparation

Pour hot water into a teacup. Add nettle and mint leaves and let steep 5–10 minutes. Strain tea to remove leaves and enjoy.

LAVENDER AND LINDEN HERBAL TEA

This calming herbal tea makes a great before-bed beverage. Lavender is often easily found in community gardens and can also be grown in your own balcony or windowsill garden. Linden, or tilia, trees are common in Europe and parts of North America, and their flowers have a calming effect when consumed. They can also help relieve nasal congestion, which is helpful at the onset of the spring allergy season! Add a touch of honey to sweeten up this subtle blend.

Ingredients

1 cup (240 mL) hot water
1 tablespoon dried or fresh linden flowers
1 tablespoon dried or fresh lavender

Preparation

Pour the boiling water into a teacup. Add linden and lavender and let steep 5–10 minutes. Strain tea and enjoy.

FINDING THE BEST BREAD IN PARIS

It may be surprising to see, upon arriving in Paris, that the cliché of Parisians heading home at night with a baguette under their arm is absolutely true. You may not see many berets or striped shirts, but the daily baguette-buying tradition is one that remains largely widespread. The French take their bread seriously, and the baguette—the most iconic of Parisian breads—is held to high standards of quality. French law states that baguettes can only be made using four ingredients: flour, a leavening agent, water, and salt. While the classic baguette remains a staple at the Parisian's dinner table (in the countryside you are much more likely to find the people buy a large loaf of bread, or *pain de campagne*, that is consumed throughout the week), a growing interest in locally sourced alternative flours, wild yeasts, and organic ingredients has brought a wider variety of breads to the city's bakeries.

Among Paris's oldest bakeries is Poilâne (8 rue Cherche Midi, 6th arrondissement), which has been around since 1932. Using stone-ground flour, sourdough starters, and fresh sea salt from Guérande in Brittany, Poilâne makes bread that has received international acclaim. You won't find a baguette

PAIN DES
AMIS

Un pain tout en croûte,
légèrement fumé.
Farine biologique.

250g / 500g
2,65€ / 5,3€

in sight in this historic bakery, but you will find crowds of tourists lured by fresh sourdough loaves, called *miches*, straight out of the wood-burning oven.

Du Pain et des Idées (34 rue Yves Toudic, 10th arrondissement) has been a corner bakery in this canal side neighborhood since 1870. The current baker, Christophe Vasseur, has respected the site's tradition, keeping the green painted ceilings and mirrored walls of the original boutique and offering only traditional baked goods that keep with the epoch. Using only organic ingredients and artisanal methods, Vasseur produces baked goods that bring Parisians and tourists from near and far. One of the most popular items, the Pain des Amis, is allowed to ferment for two days before baking, resulting in a flavorful loaf with hints of nuts and maple syrup.

Another proponent of the "slow rise" approach to bread-making is Veronique Mauclerc, whose organic bakery is home to one of the few remaining wood-burning stoves in the city. Visit La Boulangerie par Veronique Mauclerc (83 rue de Crimée, 19th arrondissement) and you will be greeted by blurry-eyed bakers who have been up since the early hours of the morning, preparing bread for its two phases of rising, the first of which lasts for one and a half hours, followed by a second fifteen-hour rise. The slow rise approach allows the bread to develop its taste, creating the slightly sour element that is so sought after by bread connoisseurs.

Paving the way in the world of gluten-free bread is a handful of adventurous bakeries. Among the first to experiment with alternate flours is Helmut Newcake (36 rue Bichat, 10th arrondissement). Made using buckwheat and chestnut-based flours, to name a few, Helmut Newcake offers gluten-, and often sugar-, lactose-, and egg-free breads and pastries. The boutique also has an épicerie where you can purchase gluten-free goods such as cereals and other products imported from some of the more gluten-free friendly countries. Thank You, My Deer (112 rue St. Maur, 11th arrondissement) is a small bakery that uses French-sourced organic corn, rice, and quinoa flour to make the baked goods that make up their sandwiches, brunches, and pastries. They also serve coffee from the excellent *Coutume Café* (page 84). Boulangerie Chambelland (14 rue Ternaux, 11th arrondissement) doesn't make a big fuss out of advertising their gluten-free baked goods, because the finished product speaks for itself. The bakery is furnished with Formica tables and a bookshelf of great foodie reading material for sale, providing a cozy place to enjoy lunch on site or to-go (takeout orders are sold at a lower price). Baker Thomas Chambelland uses rice flour that is sourced from the southern France-grown Riz de Camargue that is then milled in the region before making its way to Paris. The bread here is truly delicious and the bakery's signature *choquettes*, or sugar puffs, are quickly becoming among the city's favorites.

You don't necessarily have to go to a bakery to try some of the city's best bread. Thierry Breton, of *La Pointe du Grouin* (page 79) and its sister restaurants, Chez Casimir and Chez Michel, is also a master bread maker who delivers his loaves of pain de campagne by bike to over eighty restaurants in Paris. You can find his bread served at *En Vrac* (page 22), *Café Lomi* (page 84), *Le Grand 8* (page 22) and *Le Verre Volé* (page 20), to name a few.

If you want to have a go at making your own bread while in Paris, the progressive and always inventive suburb of Montreuil has a collective earthen oven and regularly hosts events to teach the community how to make their own bread, pizza, and pastries. The association Salut les Co-pains organizes the events, as well as seasonal markets that feature locally grown ingredients, and other gatherings throughout the year.

Fresh baked bread by Thierry Breton.

MARCHÉ ORNANO

BOULEVARD ORNANO, 75018
Mº SIMPLON (LINE 4)
OPEN: TUESDAY, FRIDAY, AND SUNDAY, 8:00 A.M.–1:00 P.M.

At the edge of the 18th arrondissement you will find Marché Ornano, which matches shouts for shoppers as ardent vendors offer exotic and imported fruits and vegetables. Among the exclamations, on the corner of boulevard Ornano and rue du Simplon you'll find Jean-Michel Delahaye's vegetable stand. The only out-right producteur at the market, Jean-Michel sells vegetables from his farm in Cergy-Pontoise, located twenty-one miles from Paris. Delahaye wasn't always the only farmer at this market. By his count, as little as ten years ago Marché Ornano hosted many more independent producers from the Île-de-France and other neighboring regions.

Jean-Michel Delahaye at Marché Ornano.

It is not without sacrifice that he himself comes to the market three days a week. The travel time, which can be over an hour with the infamous Paris traffic, compounded with the time taken away from tending to the farm while selling at the market, make it a huge undertaking for a small agricultural operation like his.

The farmer's efforts are clearly appreciated, as the locally grown vegetables at his stand draw crowds of shoppers on market days. Busy Sunday afternoons see shoppers chatting in line as they wait to be served by Jean-Michel

Shopping at Jean-Michel Delahaye's stand at Marché Ornano.

and his team. "I don't mind the wait," one woman announced on one such day, as she joined the back of the winding line. "The produce is better here. I have a friend who bought potatoes somewhere else and they just weren't the same," she confided to her neighbors in line, who nodded and clucked in agreement.

MARCHÉ MOUTON DUVERNET

PLACE JACQUES DEMY, 75014
Mº MOUTON DUVERNET (LINE 4)
OPEN: TUESDAY AND FRIDAY, 7:00 A.M.–2:30 P.M.

Tucked away on a small square in the 14th arrondissement, Marché Mouton Duvernet is one of the Left Bank's most charming markets. The *fromage*-infused air mingling with the aroma of early lunch preparations accompanies the atmosphere in this classic Parisian residential neighborhood. While most of the produce here is imported, you can count on market gardener Eric Credard for locally grown fruits and vegetables. Aside from the occasional organic lemon or other nonnative varieties to diversify the selection, the majority of Credard's products are grown on his farm. Fresh lettuce, radish, and rhubarb are common sites while doing springtime shopping at Credard's stand.

Marché Mouton Duvernet also has an organic vendor, with a wide array of produce and a friendly staff. Take advantage of being in this part of town and stop by *La Cave des Papilles* (page 19) after you've finished at the market. One of the city's most reputable natural wine shops, this *cave* is definitely worth being included in any wine lover's itinerary.

WINE TASTINGS IN PARIS AND BEYOND

Regular wine tastings occur throughout the year in Paris, but the season really picks up in the spring and summer, when warmer weather inspires wine shops to take their tasting rooms to the sidewalks. La Derniere Goutte (6 rue Bourbon de Chateau, 6th arrondissement) holds regular free wine tastings, usually on Fridays from 5–7:30 p.m. *Le Vin en Tête* (page 20) is also host to frequent free in-store wine tastings—sign up for their mailing list for regular updates on upcoming events. The historic Caves Augé (116 boulevard Haussmann, 8th arrondissement) are as famous for their free tastings as they are for their illustrious clientele (legend has it, Proust used to pick up a bottle or two for himself here back in the day). Tastings are usually held on Saturdays in late spring and early summer and can get quite crowded, so arrive early or plan on staying late if you want to have face time with the invited winemakers.

If you're interested in having a truly unique wine tasting experience, there's nothing better than visiting the winemakers in their natural habitat and touring your favorite vineyards. Many winemaking regions, such as the Loire and Champagne, are an easy day trip from Paris and the Burgundy and Languedoc-Roussillon regions make for a great wine-soaked weekend away.

Remember that the majority of natural winemakers are working small-scale vineyards and do everything from farming to fermenting to bottling largely on their own. Suffice to say, they are busy people. However, many winemakers are happy to have visitors, are proud of the work they do, and are pleased to share the fruits of their labor. Many natural winemakers will be happy to make an appointment for you to visit their vines and see how they work (preferably during the week and off-season; for example, not during the September-October harvest season).

Winemakers usually don't charge a tasting fee, and that's not the only difference from your typical tasting in North America. Don't expect a fancy tasting room or a staff pouring a predetermined selection of vintages. Most likely you will be taken around the vineyard by the winemakers themselves and taste wherever they see fit—in a wine cellar, on a picnic table, underneath a shade tree—whatever works best on that day. Since natural winemakers adapt their vintages to what nature and the seasons bring that year, they often experiment with their yearly harvest, adjusting to the grapes' personality and condition and how it reflects what happened during the growing season. This means that an on-site tasting likely holds surprises, including wines that you can't find at your local wine shop and may never taste again.

When visiting a winemaker, it is polite—and expected—that you come prepared to buy a case of wine. A *vigneron*'s time is precious, and it is customary to repay their kindness by taking bottles home with you. If traveling overseas, be sure to let your natural wines settle once they've arrived at their final destination. The myth that natural wine doesn't travel well is widespread but largely unfounded. As in life and all things natural, the secret to a good wine is harmony and balance and, after a long-distance flight, everyone needs a little time to decompress.

FAVORITE FOOD(IE) SHOPS

Paris markets offer a wide selection of fresh ingredients and on-the-go snacks, but they sometimes lack in options for taking your favorite French flavors home with you. Fortunately, the city has a handful of friendly shops stocked with a wide array of local specialties and artisanal items that make great gifts and souvenirs.

L'Epicerie Générale (43 rue de Verneuil, 7th arrondissement) is a charming left bank shop that specializes in "le beau et le bio Français." With a selection of artisanal items from regions all over France, this shop assures quality, locally sourced products. Pick up a jar of honey from Provence to prepare *Mushroom Risotto with Honey Roasted Figs* (page 42) or choose a French-made olive oil to make homemade *Vinaigrette* (page 148). The boutique also features French rice and other dried goods as well as its very own signature candles, which make unique gifts.

The friendly staff at La Boutique des Saveurs (34 rue des Petits Carreaux, 2nd arrondissement) is happy to help you make a selection from their carefully curated range of products, all of which are sourced from France's natural parks. Produced using traditional and artisanal methods, the French specialties (conserves, vinegars, mustards, spices) on offer are true expressions of French terroir and the gastronomic tradition that the country is famous for. While there, grab some Dijon mustard for a *Tangy Tomato Mustard Tart* (page 192) or a selection of dried herbs to make *Five Herb Baked Tomatoes* (page 178).

The most recent outpost of local favorite and ingredient-focused restaurant *Le Verre Volé* (page 20) is L'Epicerie du Verre Volé (54 rue de la Folie Méricourt, 11th arrondissement), which continues in the tradition of sourcing exceptional ingredients. The small shop is equipped with a deli counter that sells charcuterie, cheeses, and a constantly changing spread of sandwich options. A great spot to stock up for a picnic, you can also find a selection of French-made products here. Choose from the infused vinegars that you can use to experiment with new spins on classic salad dressings. The shop also has a wide range of dried goods, including beans, pasta, and French lentils.

The local-minded and quality-conscious corner store Causses (55 rue Notre Dame de Lorette, 9th arrondissement) stocks fresh seasonal fruits and vegetables (with a selection of Île-de-France–grown items) along with French specialty ingredients and products including charcuterie, cheese, conserves, and candies. Artisan alcohols are also on offer, with a selection of ciders to accompany your *Apple Cider Steamed Mussels* (page 156) and liquors that can be used when mixing up a round of *Kirs* (page 170). For lunch, check out La Fabrique next door, where a meal can be enjoyed on site or to-go.

The rue du Nil, a street which is quickly becoming the site of locavore pilgrimages, is home to Terroirs d'Avenir (7 rue du Nil, 2nd arrondissement), an innovative enterprise comprised of three boutiques—a butcher, fishmonger, and general store—all offering high-quality ingredients from the finest producers. At the butcher you will find the vrai jambon de Paris for your *"Prince of Paris" Grilled Cheese Sandwich* (page 40). Cross the street and mingle with local chefs and conscientious shoppers at the general store, which sells fresh vegetables along with a superb selection of natural wines and fancy pantry items including pastas, herbs, spices, and conserves.

La Recolte (18 Boulevard des Batignolles, 17th arrondissement) is a great place to stop after doing a tour of *Marché Biologique des Batignolles* (page 119). Here you will find seasonal produce, specialty products, and nonperishables, all with a story. The shop proudly shares the origins of their products by posting biographies of the people behind your peaches and *Fish Soup* (page 30). Mathieu Mulliez, the engaged owner of this shop, is committed to bringing the best French products to the customer, including a lovely selection of infused oils and vinegars, beers, and locally milled flours. The constantly changing selection of fruits and vegetables is exciting and of excellent quality, and can be enjoyed on site in the shop's fresh pressed juices.

In addition to these independent boutiques, Paris also has a variety of more traditional grocery stores that offer organic produce. Subsidiaries of

larger grocery chains—like Naturalia, which is owned by *supermarché* giant Monoprix, and Bio C' Bon—are springing up around the city, offering organic options in a supermarket setting. These stores may be ubiquitous and convenient to shop at, but they are less engaged in supporting local farmers and small-scale farms. If you want to avoid giving your money to corporations who are riding the organic wave, there are several alternatives that are fun to discover and explore.

The Biocoop collective regroups a network of stores that are owned by independent, militant, and engaged actors in the local food movement. Their charter requires each member store to cooperate with and further develop the cause of sustainable organic agriculture all while working in partnership with producers, associations, and organic certification agencies and their labels. Some exceptional biocoops include Le Retour à La Terre Rive Gauche (1 rue le Goff, 5th arrondissement) and Canal Bio (46 Quai de la Loire, 19th arrondissement).

SPRING RECIPES

APPETIZERS, SIDES, SALADS, AND SOUPS

BAKED EGGS WITH FRESH CHIVES / *OEUFS COCOTTE*

This recipe makes a simple entrée for lunch or dinner as well as a delightful egg addition to brunch. Chopped chives add a dash of color to this almost effortless French classic, which is easy to serve in individual ramekins. This has become a breakfast staple in my home, where I use fresh eggs from the *Marché Biologique des Batignolles* (page 119) to whip up a breakfast dish that is sure to please and start the day off right.

Ingredients

For each 3-inch (7½ cm) ramekin:
Butter to coat the inside of the ramekin
1 tablespoon crème fraîche
1 large egg
Generous pinch of grated Gruyère
Salt and pepper to taste
Chopped fresh chives to garnish

Preparation

Preheat oven to 375°F (190°C). Butter the inside of each ramekin. Add crème fraîche, then crack one egg into each ramekin, without breaking the yolk. Top with grated Gruyère and a dash of salt and pepper. Place on middle rack in oven (if making several, place on a baking sheet). Bake for 6–8 minutes, until cheese is melted and eggs are set but not cooked through. The yolk should look glassy and remain still when ramekin is lightly shaken. Sprinkle with chopped chives and serve in ramekin with toasted baguette.

STEAMED ASPARAGUS WITH HOLLANDAISE SAUCE / ASPERGES SAUCE HOLLANDAISE

This easy spring recipe brings together lightly steamed asparagus with delicate, buttery *Hollandaise* (page 38). In France, you will typically find white asparagus, which has a thicker and tougher stalk than the green asparagus more common in the United States. If you are using green asparagus in place of white, reduce the steam time. You can also add steamed baby potatoes to give more substance to this side dish, or any other young spring vegetables that you find at the market.

Ingredients

Serves 4

2 medium bunches (about 600 grams) asparagus (white or green—adjust steam time depending), washed and with tough ends cut or snapped off (if the stalks are very tough, use a vegetable peeler to remove outer skin)

Hollandaise Sauce (page 38)

Optional: 3 cups (300 grams) baby potatoes, or other young spring vegetables, peeled and roughly chopped

Preparation

Fill a large pot halfway with water and bring to a boil. Add asparagus (and spring vegetables, if using them) in a steamer basket and cover. Steam for 13–15 minutes (5–7 minutes if using green asparagus) until slightly tender. Remove from heat and let cool. Arrange on separate plates and drizzle with hollandaise sauce. Serve immediately.

MARCHÉ BATIGNOLLES POTATO PANCAKES / GALETTES DE POMME DE TERRE

It's always dangerous to go food shopping on an empty stomach, which is why the potato pancake stand at *Marché Biologique des Batignolles* (page 119) is often my first stop at the market. Hot off the griddle, these simple potato patties are always worth the wait and are part of many a market-goer's morning ritual.

Ingredients

Makes about a dozen pancakes
6 medium-sized russet potatoes
   (about 2 pounds / 2½ kilo),
   peeled and grated
3 medium-sized eggs
1 medium onion, thinly sliced
¼ cup (30 grams) grated Gruyère
Salted butter
1 teaspoon nutmeg
Salt and pepper to taste

Preparation

Wash, peel, and grate potatoes. Pat dry with a paper towel or dish towel to absorb excess liquid. In a medium bowl, mix dry, grated potatoes with eggs, chopped onion, cheese, nutmeg, and a dash of salt and pepper. In a large pan or griddle, melt 1 tablespoon salted butter on medium-high heat. Form the potato mixture into small balls, making about 12 in total. Flatten the balls making patties that are about ½-¼ inch (1 cm) thick. In batches, add to heated pan and let cook for about 2–3 minutes on each side, until both sides are golden brown. Press to flatten as you cook the patties and preserve in a warm place, like the oven or a covered dish, and continue to fry the remaining potato pancakes. Add more butter to the pan as necessary between batches. Serve hot, seasoning with salt before serving.

ARTICHOKES WITH GARDENER'S VINAIGRETTE / ARTICHAUTS AU VINAIGRETTE

Jean-Michel at *Marché Ornano* (page 132) always has the most beautiful spring artichokes. I switch between the lovely little lavender ones and the large green globes that I bring home and steam at least once a week during the springtime. A steamed artichoke with *Gardener's Vinaigrette* (page 151) makes great starter for a simple meal. If you're looking for a more filling accompaniment, pair your artichoke with fresh homemade *Aioli* (page 146).

Ingredients

Serves 2
1 large artichoke
1 dried bay leaf
2 cloves of garlic, whole, with
    skin
½ lemon
1 tablespoon extra virgin olive oil
1 pinch sea salt

Preparation

Wash the artichoke and cut off the top ½ inch (1 cm) of the leaves along with the bottom of the stem, leaving about ½ inch (1 cm) at the base of the artichoke. Place the artichoke in a medium pot and then fill with cold water until the artichoke is halfway submerged. Add bay leaf, whole garlic cloves, lemon, olive oil, and sea salt, and bring water to a boil. Reduce heat to a simmer and place a cover on the pot. Cook for 45–60 minutes, adding water as necessary. The cooking time will depend on the size of the artichoke, so after cooking for about 40 minutes, check artichoke regularly. The artichoke is done when the outside leaves can be easily removed and the flesh is tender. Drain the water and let the artichoke cool until no warmer than room temperature. Serve with vinaigrette or aioli as a dipping sauce. Don't forget to provide empty bowls to hold eaten leaves.

AIOLI

This garlicky spin on a basic mayonnaise is easy to prepare and can be done in advance, as it gets better after being left in the fridge for a few hours. Be sure to use eggs that are at room temperature to get the right emulsion and consistency. Once you've mastered this recipe you'll never buy mayonnaise in the store again!

Ingredients

1 egg yolk, at room temperature
1 teaspoon Dijon mustard
2 cloves of garlic, crushed
½ cup (120 mL) extra virgin olive oil

Preparation

In a small bowl, whisk together egg yolk, mustard, and garlic until mixture become slightly creamy and light yellow in color, about 2–3 minutes. Slowly add olive oil in a thin stream while continuing to whisk. The consistency should remain creamy and color should slowly lighten as the oil is whisked in. Continue to slowly add oil, making sure the aioli remains thick. Stop adding oil if the mixture becomes too thin, or begins to have an oily texture or taste. Once aioli sticks to the whisk, cover the bowl with plastic wrap and keep in the refrigerator for at least one hour before serving. Aioli can be kept for 3-5 days in the refrigerator.

FIRST SIGN OF SPRING CUCUMBER SALAD / SALADE DE CONCOMBRES À LA CRÈME FRAÎCHE

This salad is great for a picnic or as a side dish. The combination of shallots and cucumbers with a light dressing of crème fraîche and lemon is refreshing and allows the crispness of seasonal cucumbers to shine.

Ingredients

Serves 4

¾ cup (180 mL) crème fraîche
2 shallots, diced
Juice from one lemon
2 tablespoons chopped chives
2 large cucumbers, peeled and
  thinly sliced
Salt
Freshly ground black pepper

Preparation

In a salad bowl, stir together crème fraîche, shallots, lemon juice, and chives until combined. Add cucumbers and toss until coated in crème fraîche dressing. Add salt and freshly ground pepper to taste. Serve immediately or keep in the refrigerator, covered, before serving.

SAUCE

VINAIGRETTES (CLASSIC, DIJON, AND GARDENER'S VINAIGRETTE)

While you can find bottles of *sauce salade* gathering dust on the shelves of French supermarkets, after you've seen the ease with which the locals whip up delicious vinaigrette, you'll wonder why anyone would ever buy something that is so easily made at home. French vinaigrettes follow a simple formula, but also leave room for experimentation. Start with 1 part vinegar to 2 parts oil and always dissolve salt or an acidic element into the vinegar before adding oil. Incorporate additional ingredients or substitute flavored vinegars and oils for a personalized dressing that brings out the flavor of the locally grown lettuce that can be found at the market all year long. Here are a few of my favorite variations:

CLASSIC VINAIGRETTE

This vinaigrette can be made with any vinegar—I particularly enjoy walnut-infused vinegar—and olive oil. The shallots are optional, but add a nice touch when making a simple lettuce and vinaigrette side salad. This will make enough for one medium-sized head of lettuce; increase ingredients proportionally for larger salads.

Ingredients

1 tablespoon balsamic vinegar
1 teaspoon salt
2 tablespoons extra virgin olive oil
1 medium shallot, chopped

Preparation

Pour 1 tablespoon vinegar into a large salad bowl. Add salt and whisk together. Continue whisking while slowly adding oil. Add shallots and stir to combine. Add salad to the bowl and toss.

DIJON VINAIGRETTE

Dijon substitutes the salt in this recipe, making for stronger vinaigrette that goes well with steamed vegetables such as cabbage or leeks. This will make enough for one medium-sized head of lettuce or a vegetable dish for two people; increase ingredients proportionally for larger salads.

Ingredients

1 tablespoon balsamic vinegar
2 teaspoons Dijon mustard
2 tablespoons extra virgin olive oil
1 pinch tarragon, chopped or dried (optional)

Preparation

Pour vinegar into a bowl, add Dijon mustard, and whisk together. Once a creamy consistency is reached, slowly whisk in olive oil. Whisk together until combined. Add tarragon and then toss with salad or serve as a sauce over steamed vegetables.

GARDENER'S VINAIGRETTE

This recipe is inspired from a French cookbook that was published in the 1920s. The recipe assumes that we all have access to gardens with a selection of fresh herbs. While this may not often be the case for Parisians (or city dwellers in general), I think it is possible to manage growing a few easy herbs on a balcony or windowsill. If you get herbs such as basil, cilantro, and parsley from the market, keep them fresh in the fridge by arranging them in an herb vase. Fill a glass or jar with water (enough to immerse about halfway up the stem) and place your fresh herbs inside. If you want to keep the herbs for longer than 3–5 days this way, cover them with a plastic bag to extend their shelf life for as long as 2 weeks.

Use whatever you have on hand to freshen up this vinaigrette, which works great as a dipping sauce with a *Steamed Artichoke* (page 145) or simply tossed with a salad of baby greens.

Ingredients

1 tablespoon balsamic vinegar
1 teaspoon salt
2 tablespoons extra virgin olive oil
1–2 tablespoons fresh herbs such as thyme, parsley, chives, and tarragon

Preparation

Pour 1 tablespoon vinegar into a bowl. Add salt and whisk together. Continue whisking while slowly adding oil. Add fresh herbs and stir to combine. Toss with a salad or serve as a dip with steamed artichokes.

MAINS

PARCHMENT BAKED SEA BASS EN PAPILLOTE WITH SPRING VEGETABLES / BAR EN PAPILLOTE AUX LÉGUMES DE PRINTEMPS

Sea bass is often seen on menus across France, as it is found in many of the country's coastal waters. This simple method of preparation pairs young spring vegetables with fresh fish, wrapped up in an easy-to-serve parcel. The papillotes, or envelopes, can be prepared hours in advance and kept in the refrigerator until dinnertime, making this a perfect plan-ahead recipe for a weeknight meal or dinner party.

Ingredients

Serves 4
4–5 cups (750 grams) mixed
  spring vegetables (such as
  turnips, carrots, radish, or
  new potatoes), thinly sliced
4 sea bass fillets
4 tablespoons fresh parsley,
  roughly chopped
Salt and pepper to taste
½ cup (120 mL) extra virgin olive
  oil
Juice from 1 lemon

Preparation

Preheat oven to 375°F (190°C). Prepare your papillote by rolling out pieces of tinfoil that are a little more than twice the size of your sea bass fillet. Prepare one piece of tinfoil for each fillet. Fold up the edges of the square of tinfoil, as if making a baking sheet. The edges should be thick in order to hold the ingredients, so create sturdy walls by folding the tinfoil twice around the edges. Brush the inside of the envelope with olive oil.

In a bowl, mix spring vegetables together and then distribute them evenly among the bottom half of each envelope, making a bed for the sea bass. Lay a fillet on top of vegetables in each envelope and sprinkle with parsley and a dash of salt and pepper. Cover each fillet in about 2 tablespoons of olive oil each and then top with an even distribution of fresh squeezed lemon juice.

Close the packets by folding the empty half over the portion containing the fillet. Close tightly, crimping tinfoil together, making sure the seams are sealed and will not leak. Place papillotes on a baking sheet and bake on the middle rack of the oven for 35–40 minutes. Serve hot, either in the papillote or removed from tinfoil, with a side of rice.

SPRING CHICKEN WITH ASPARAGUS / POULET AUX ASPERGES DE ST-CLAUDE

This recipe is inspired by a recipe for Poulet aux Asperges de St-Claude that I found in a magazine from the early sixties, dedicated to the Loir-et-Cher region in France, where I have spent time harvesting and pruning in the grapevines. The large white asparagus from this region are sautéed and paired with chicken in a creamy sauce in this perfect main dish for a Sunday lunch.

Ingredients

Serves 4

2 large bunches asparagus
    (1 kilo), washed with tough
    ends removed, then chopped
    in 1 inch (2½ cm) pieces
    (white or green asparagus will
    both work)
1½ tablespoon (20 grams) butter
4 medium boneless and skinless
    chicken breasts
1 medium shallot, minced
2 cups (130 grams) button
    mushrooms, sliced
½ tablespoon fresh taragon
1 cup (240 mL) dry white wine
¾ cup (180 mL) crème fraîche
Salt and pepper
2–3 tablespoons fresh chopped
    parsley

Preparation

In a large pot, bring salted water to a boil. Add chopped asparagus, all but the points, to boiling water. Boil for five minutes, then add the asparagus points and boil for another five minutes. Drain asparagus and set aside. Melt butter in a large skillet on medium heat. Lightly salt and pepper chicken breasts, then place in skillet and cook until evenly browned, about 4–6 minutes on each side. Set chicken aside, covering to keep warm. In the same skillet, add shallot and cook about 3–5 minutes. Add mushrooms and taragon and cook another five minutes. Add wine, increase heat to medium-high, and cook until liquid reduces by about a third. Stir in asparagus. Add cream, bring to a light simmer, and cook for 3–5 minutes, until desired taste and consistency is reached. Salt and pepper to taste once removed from heat. Serve asparagus and mushroom mixture in equal parts on plates, topping with chicken breasts and garnishing with freshly chopped parsley. Serve immediately.

QUICK COD WITH SORREL SAUCE /
CABILLAUD SAUCE À L'OSEILLE

This dish is everything I love about French cuisine: fresh, simple, and buttery! An easy and impressive meal for a dinner party—think of serving with steamed new potatoes or other freshly harvested spring vegetables.

Ingredients

Serves 4

2 pounds (1 kilo) / 4 fillets of cod
   or other white fish
2 tablespoons (30 grams) salted
   butter
Salt and pepper

For the sauce:

3 tablespoons (45 grams) salted
   butter
1 medium shallot, minced
3 medium sorrel leaves,
   julienned
¾ cup (180 mL) heavy cream
Salt and pepper

Preparation

Preheat oven to 425°F (220°C). Wash and dry fish fillets and arrange in a baking dish. In a small saucepan, melt 2 tablespoons (30 grams) salted butter. Brush both sides of each fish fillet with melted butter, coating evenly. Sprinkle each fillet lightly with salt and pepper and place on a tinfoil-lined baking dish on the middle rack of the oven. Bake fish for 10–15 minutes and then turn on broiler for an additional 2–3 minutes, or until fish turns golden.

In the meantime, make the sauce. Melt butter in a saucepan on medium heat. Add shallots and sorrel and let cook 3–5 minutes, or until sorrel starts to wilt. Slowly stir in cream and continue to stir over heat until sauce thickens slightly. Salt and pepper to taste. Pour over baked cod and serve immediately.

APPLE CIDER STEAMED MUSSELS WITH HOMEMADE FRIES / MOULES AU CIDRE ET FRITES MAISON

Quick trips to Normandy are a Parisian's go-to respite from the stress of the city. If you can't hop on a train or don't have Normandy as your neighbor, this easy dish brings together the best of the *terroir* (and *meroir*!) of this lovely seaside region to your table. Try to find artisanal apple cider for a crisp addition to these classic steamed mussels.

Ingredients

For the mussels:
Serves 4
6 pounds (3 kilos) mussels
2 tablespoons extra virgin olive
    oil
1 large yellow onion, diced
2 cups (480 mL) dry apple cider
4 tablespoons fresh parsley,
    chopped

Preparation

Thoroughly wash and de-beard mussels by scrubbing or cutting away any threads that remain. Remove any mussels that are already open or have broken shells. In a large pot, heat olive oil on medium heat and sauté onion until transparent, about 3–5 minutes. Stir in mussels until lightly coated in oil. Add cider and cover pot. Increase temperature to medium-high and cook until mussels open their shells, about 5–10 minutes. Divide mussels into individual bowls, garnishing each with fresh parsley. Serve with homemade fries and extra empty bowls for discarded shells.

Ingredients

For the fries:
5 large russet potatoes
Vegetable oil to coat potatoes and
    baking sheet
Salt

Preparation

Preheat oven to 425°F (220°C). Julienne potatoes into large sticks—these should be thicker than shoestring fries and all uniform in size. Toss potato sticks in a large bowl with enough vegetable oil to coat them evenly. Use a paper towel with a dab of vegetable oil to coat a baking sheet, and then spread potatoes out in one layer, avoiding overlap. If potatoes remain, set aside for a second batch. Sprinkle with salt and bake for 30 minutes, flipping them over after 15 minutes to bake evenly on both sides. Remove and let cool before serving.

DESSERTS

RHUBARB COMPOTE AND YOGURT PARFAIT / *COMPOTE DE RHUBARBE AVEC YAOURT*

This recipe comes directly from the ladies in line at Jean-Michel Delahaye's stand at *Marché Ornano* (page 132), where a lively debate was had about just what to do with rhubarb. After much discussion, we came to a consensus that a thick rhubarb compote to be used in tarts or over yogurt was the best way to put this spring stalk to use.

Ingredients

Makes about 3 cups (700 grams)
4 cups (525 grams) rhubarb, chopped
¼ cup (50 grams) unrefined sugar
½ cup (120 mL) water
1 cup (250 grams) yogurt per person
Fresh mint

Preparation

Wash rhubarb stalks and remove the skin by using a paring knife, lightly cutting into the stalk and peeling back the skin in strips. Do this wherever the skin is hard and needs to be removed (not all the skin needs to be peeled off, just the rough parts). If the stalks are young, there may not be much hard skin to remove, and stalks can be left as they are. Cut the skinned rhubarb into ¾-inch (2 cm) pieces.

In a bowl, combine the rhubarb with sugar. Mix and let sit for at least 45 minutes, while the sugar extracts juice from the rhubarb. In a medium pot, bring water to a boil. Add the rhubarb and sugar mixture and bring to a boil again. Reduce heat, bringing water to a simmer. Cover and let cook 5 minutes. Remove cover and let cook another 8–10 minutes. Use a wooden spoon to stir and break up bigger pieces of rhubarb while cooking.

Once the compote has a liquid consistency, with not too many large pieces of rhubarb (some larger bits can be kept as they will add texture to your compote), remove from heat and let cool. Once cooled, transfer to a glass container or mason jar and seal firmly. Compote can be stored in the refrigerator for up to one week. Using individual-sized parfait dishes, or any large, clear glass (such as a wine glass or stout water glass), create layers with yogurt and rhubarb compote, starting with yogurt then alternating with compote. Garnish with fresh mint leaves and serve immediately.

STRAWBERRIES AND CIDER /
FRAISES DE BOIS AU CIDRE

This is an unbelievably simple but perfect-for-spring recipe that I first tried at *La Pointe du Grouin* (page 79). Small wild strawberries are the perfect size for this dessert, but normal size halved strawberries will also do the trick. Try to get a good artisanal apple cider so as not to overwhelm the palette with too much sweetness. It doesn't get much easier than this recipe, which is simply served in individual wine glasses.

Ingredients

For each person:
½ cup (75 grams) wild strawberries, or 6 regular strawberries, halved
1 cup (240 mL) dry apple cider
Fresh mint, chopped

Preparation

Wash strawberries, and cut in half if using larger berries. Place strawberries in a large wine glass or parfait dish and pour cider over them. Sprinkle with chopped fresh mint leaves and serve immediately.

CHOCOLATE MOUSSE / *MOUSSE AU CHOCOLAT*

Spring is a season of chocolate in Paris. Throughout the month of April, window fronts of bakeries and chocolate shops fill up with iconic spring symbols transformed into chocolate. Easter eggs are ubiquitous and chocolate fish, representing the *poisson d'avril*—an April Fools' Day joke that involves sticking a paper fish on the back of your friends and teachers—tempt shoppers with a sweet tooth. Well-known chocolatiers take this time of year as a sort of challenge, creating extravagent displays of their expertly crafted chocolate creations, but you can celebrate the chocolate season at home with this simple mousse recipe.

Ingredients

Serves 4–6

3½ tablespoons (50 grams) unsalted butter

¾ cup (250 grams / 9 ounces) semisweet chocolate

6 medium eggs

¼ cup (50 grams) + 1 tablespoon granulated sugar

Preparation

Bring a large pot of water to boil. In a smaller saucepan, create a *bain mairie* and melt butter and chocolate together, stirring regularly. Set aside chocolate and butter to cool to room temperature. Separate the eggs, keeping 4 egg yolks and 6 egg whites. In a large bowl, whisk egg whites until they start to thicken, add 1 tablespoon sugar, and beat until they form peaks. Stir egg yolks into room temperature chocolate mixture, and continue to stir until egg yolks are fully incorporated and mixture has a thin, liquid consistency. Slowly fold half of egg white mixture into chocolate. Pour the chocolate mixture into the bowl of beaten egg whites. Fold mixture together until fully incorporated; be sure to mix well while keeping the mousse fluffy. Cover bowl with plastic wrap and refrigerate for at least one hour before serving. Mousse can be prepared for individual servings by preparing separate parfait dishes or cups before refrigerating, or it can be served directly from the bowl.

SUMMER

Summer sees a population shift in Paris, when locals steadily abandon ship for sunnier vacation spots while tourists flock to the city. Paris life continues at a slower, calmer pace, and this season remains one of the best times to explore side streets and settle into a sunny *terrasse*. The demand for fresh vegetables also remains high and local vendors and their seasonal vegetables can be found at markets until mid-July, when some of the farmers take their yearly holiday. Restaurants and wine stores begin to close for the season, so be sure to call ahead and confirm they are open—many favorite addresses will close down for their *congé annuel* in July and August. *Paris by Mouth* (page 77) puts together a list every year of the annual closures of favorite restaurants, as well as which ones stay open throughout the summer.

Markets make a great first stop for a day spent *sous le soleil*. Stock your picnic basket with easy snacks like rosy radishes and a mix of fresh berries and head to one of the city's parks to enjoy a picnic and people watching.

In Season: *bell peppers, black currants, blueberries, carrots, cherries, eggplant, fennel, green beans, radishes, rhubarbs, sorrels, summer squash, tomatoes*

MARCHÉ RASPAIL

BOULEVARD RASPAIL, 75006
Mᵒ RENNES (LINE 12)
OPEN: SUNDAY, 9:00 A.M.–2:00 P.M.

Another one of Paris's all-organic markets, Marché Raspail, is snugly set up along the boulevard Raspail in the posh 6th arrondissement. A favorite among well-to-do American expats and their impeccably sophisticated neighbors, this market is great for people watching as well as food shopping. Many of the vendors you will find here can also be found at  Marché Biologique des Batignolles, but there are also unique discoveries to be made, including Eric Refour's stand, where you will find a rotating rainbow of apple varieties that shift with the changing of the seasons, and O'Regal Muffins, purveyor of locally sourced, golden brown English muffins and other baked goods. Stop by and say hello to Valérie, who will serve you a coffee to go while you choose among her famous muffins, scones, and *gâteaux*.

C'Bio is stocked with vegetables from both local production and abroad. The friendly staff here is helpful and full of suggestions for new fruits to try. The selection of locally grown produce comes from Île-de-France and is fresh and fabulous. Stock up on your veggies, and then stop for freshly laid eggs from La Ferme du Nohain. The ever-charming sales team, made up of Isabelle and Benjamin, is proud of their magnificent eggs, sourced from the 1,200 chickens on their farm in Burgundy. Sold in three sizes (small, medium, large) and by the half or full dozen, this is the best address for eggs in the entire city. Isabelle and Benjamin also have a stand at *Marché Biologique des Batignolles* (page 119) and Marché Biologique des Lilas (avenue Waldeck Rousseau, Les Lilas), just outside of Paris.

VALÉRIE DEBIAIS: THE MUFFIN MADAME

The food truck trend (page 7) hit Paris a few years ago, but Valérie Debiais's husband, Michael Healey, set the bar for four-wheeled food trends back in 2005 when he first brought his famous muffin mobile to Marché Raspail. Equipped with a wood-burning oven, Michael's O'Regal Muffins brought fresh baked goods to adoring fans and quickly became an institution at this neighborhood market. The business expanded when Valérie (who met Michael at the market) joined in the muffin fun, eventually taking over market duty in 2007.

While the muffin truck wore out years ago, its original oven is still used for making the duo's famous treats. All the baking is done at the couple's home, using both a traditional and four-wheeled kitchen. The baked goods are then brought to the market using a more conventional mode of transport—Valérie's trusty minivan.

Valérie has since added new *patisseries* to the O'Regal product line, mixing traditional anglo favorites, such as their famed English muffins, with more French fare including delicate *canelés*. The O'Regal stand is a regular pit stop for Raspail shoppers, who stop to have a morning *café* or *chocolat chaud* with a freshly baked muffin or brownie.

Not only is Valérie dedicated to using organic ingredients in her home bakery, she is also committed to sourcing locally milled flour from a producer located five miles from her home in the Loire Valley. Using organically farmed wheat, the flour is milled on site using artisanal methods.

MARCHÉ MONGE

PLACE MONGE, 75005
M° PLACE MONGE (LINE 7)
OPEN: WEDNESDAY, FRIDAY, AND SUNDAY, 7:00 A.M.–1:00 P.M.

The tiny Place Monge is home to this 5th arrondissement market three days a week. As students rush to early morning classes and the surrounding shops and restaurants slowly open their shutters and set up their sidewalk terrasses, the vendors at Marché Monge are already hard at work. The familiar smells of roast chicken, fresh fish, and aged cheese welcome shoppers as they make their way through the crowded aisles.

Shopping at Marc Mascetti's stand at Marché Monge.

Among the market stands you will find two local farmers, Marc Mascetti and Patrick Messant, both bringing fresh fruits and vegetables from their Île-de-France farms. Mascetti's farm, which is only about twenty miles south of Paris, is home to many lesser-known vegetables, which Marc takes pride in cultivating. While his stand will stock your standard selection of seasonal vegetables such as beets, carrots, and potatoes, it is often the source of culinary discovery. This friendly producteur enjoys sharing seeds with fellow farmers and experimenting with new vegetable varieties. While other farmers might content themselves with a healthy harvest of sunchokes, Marc grows both the well-known *topinambour* (sunchoke) as well as its long-lost cousin, the *crône*—a less-attractive member of the same family that would otherwise be extinct were it not for people like Marc who continue to cultivate it. Regulars at Marché Monge stop by Marc's stand to see what surprises he has in store, as well as to have a chat and a laugh before getting on with their day. More adventurous shoppers even head home with their very own bag of *crônes*. You can also find Marc at Marché Port-Royal, also in the 5th arrondissement (boulevard de Port-Royal).

MARCHÉ BIOLOGIQUE BRANCUSI

PLACE CONSTANTIN BRANCUSI, 75014
M° GAÎTÉ (LINE 13)
OPEN: SATURDAY, 9:00 A.M.–3:00 P.M.

The sleepiest of Paris's organic markets, Marché Biologique Brancusi is often overlooked when it comes to rounding up addresses for organic produce in the capital. Despite the fact that there are no independent farmers at this market, it is still worth stopping by if you're in the neighborhood. Covering the bases with a fishmonger, butcher, baker, and plenty of produce stands, you can find almost everything that you need at Marché Brancusi, and all certified organic.

The friendly vendors here are happy to let you sample their products, and the buzz of regulars chatting with neighbors and favorite market personalities creates a welcoming environment. Visit Patrick Vincent for fresh baked goods, using organic flour made from both wheat and spelt. Jacques Goupille (located across from the fishmonger) brings a wide array of produce, including wild mushrooms and sweet potatoes.

INTRO TO *APÉROS*

L'heure de l'apéro is a favorite time of day in France, commemorating the transition between the day's events and the evening meal—although many among us are likely guilty of an early afternoon *apéro* while *en vacances*. The aperitif hour includes wine or a simple cocktail and a selection of snacks to be enjoyed while winding down after a long day and taking time to converse with friends and family. The apéro is such an adored tradition that an extended version exists. Known as the *apéro dinatoire*, this type of soirée skips the table service, and has hosts providing a larger spread than your typical apéro and inviting guests to enjoy a sort of open-house ambience in an informal setting that can last from early evening well into the night.

During summertime, lighter beverages are served for the apéro, such as a glass of white or sparkling wine. If you're in the south of France you'll surely be offered pastis, and in the north you'll likely come across an apple-based liqueur, but the most universally common summer aperitif is the classic kir. Traditionally the recipe calls for a half shot of a crème de cassis topped off in a wine glass or champagne flute with Bourgogne Aligoté. Many variations of the kir exist: the Kir Royale, which replaces the white wine with champagne, and the Kir Normand, which substitutes cider for wine, are two favorite spins on the French classic.

Black currant, peach, and blackberry liqueurs or syrups can be interchangeably used in this cocktail, as can any other fruit syrup that strikes you. Summer markets are often overflowing with berries and fruits that can easily be made into simple syrups for summer kirs and cocktails.

HOMEMADE SYRUPS AND SHRUBS
FOR SEASONAL COCKTAILS

BLACK CURRANT SYRUP

Black currant syrup, or *sirop de cassis*, is a favorite nonalcoholic addition to refreshing drinks during a summer apèro. The most common
syrup to make a classic kir, as well as a perfect addition to a glass of
champagne for added fruity flavor, this simple syrup is a staple for any
French, or francophile, bar.

Ingredients

2 cups (400 grams) unrefined sugar
4 cups (960 mL) water
2 cups (250 grams) fresh black currants, washed and drained
Juice from one half lemon

Preparation

In a saucepan, stir to dissolve sugar in water, then bring to a boil. Add black
currants and lemon juice and bring to a boil again. Reduce heat to medium and
cook for 10–15 minutes, using a wooden spoon occasionally to crush the berries,
getting them to release their juices. Remove from heat and strain into a glass jar.
Let cool and then refrigerate for up to one week.

RHUBARB AND ROSEMARY SYRUP

This simple syrup marries the subtle flavors of rhubarb and rosemary.
Add it to champagne or white wine for an easy apéro drink or get creative with a rum-based cocktail such as *The Fifth Season* (page 172).

Ingredients

1½ cups (300 grams) unrefined sugar
4 cups (960 mL) water
2½ cups (300 grams) rhubarb, skin removed and cut into 1-inch (2½ cm) pieces
2–3 large sprigs of fresh rosemary

Preparation

Stir sugar into water to dissolve and bring to a boil. Add rhubarb and decrease to a
simmer. Let cook 10–15 minutes, stirring occasionally to break down the rhubarb.

After the rhubarb has cooked for about 5 minutes add rosemary sprigs and continue to simmer another 10–15 minutes, or until rhubarb is broken down and syrup tastes sweet enough. Strain the mixture to extract syrup.

BLUEBERRY AND LEMON ZEST SHRUB

Shrubs, also known as drinking vinegars, are a great way to preserve summer fruits, especially berries. Soaking blueberries in vinegar results in a sharp syrup that is great in cocktails and nonalcoholic beverages, too!

Ingredients

2½ cups (300 grams) fresh blueberries
1 cup (200 grams) unrefined sugar
Zest of 2 lemons
¼ cup (60 mL) apple cider vinegar

Preparation

Mix together blueberries, sugar, and lemon zest in a sealable jar and store in fridge for at least 24 hours, shaking occasionally. After 24 hours, strain juice off the berries, getting as much liquid as possible. Mix blueberry and lemon juice with apple cider vinegar in a sealable container. Let vinegar mixture sit in the fridge for about 3 days, or until vinegar mellows to desired taste.

THE FIFTH SEASON

This cocktail was created by Forest Collins of 52 Martinis. Based on the theme of stretching out the summer, Forest used rum, a splash of *Blueberry and Lemon Zest Shrub*, and ginger beer for a perky cocktail that makes you long for an extra season of summer.

Ingredients

2 oz dark rum
½ oz *Blueberry and Lemon Zest Shrub* (see above)
3 large ice cubes
Dash ginger beer
Lemon zest

Preparation

Shake rum and shrub with ice. Serve in a martini glass straight up, topped with a dash of ginger beer and garnished with a small slice of lemon zest.

MARCHÉ SAXE-BRETEUIL

AVENUE DE SAXE, 75007
M° SÉGUR (LINE 10)
OPEN: THURSDAY AND SATURDAY, 7:00 A.M.–2:30 P.M.

The postcard-perfect Marché Saxe-Breteuil is located in full view of the Eiffel Tower in an affluent neighborhood of the 7th arrondissement. The only open-air market to serve this sleepy section of the Left Bank, Marché Saxe-Breteuil takes itself seriously and brings with it an overwhelming selection of fresh produce, fish, meat, and dairy as well as cooking supplies and textiles. Weekdays at the market are calmer, while Saturday sees the aisles of the Avenue de Saxe liven up with both shoppers and vendors in full attendance.

Perusing a Paris market can sometimes be a passive experience; at some market stands you don't even touch your vegetables before they're put in your bag, allowing the vendor to use their better judgment and pick out produce based on ripeness and when you plan to eat it. At the Le Trepied stand at Marché Saxe-Breteuil, however, the market experience becomes much more interactive. Here the staff is friendly, following the example of charismatic salesperson Salah Lemaire. Specializing in heirloom varieties, much of Le Trepied's produce leads to a "c'est quoi ça?" questioning and several follow-up questions in line. Salah is happy to respond to inquiries into the origins or best way to prepare anything at his stand, from salsify to chou fleur. Gladly passing out samples to curious customers, Salah shares his extensive knowledge about each vegetable and inspires conversation among shoppers.

Le Trepied's farm is located in the Loiret region of France, just outside the Île-de-France. Two to three Île-de-France farmers are present at the market on the weekend, but Salah and his staff make a point of being at Marché Saxe-Breteuil on Thursdays and Saturdays, with appreciative shoppers waiting in line for their fresh fruits and vegetables on both days.

DRINK LOCAL: CRAFT BEER COMES TO PARIS

In 2014, Paris hosted its first ever "Paris Beer Week," with brewers from the Île-de-France region representing a growing number of local brewers bringing craft beer to Paris. In the years leading up to this event, spots for enjoying local microbrews have flourished, with the popularity of beer bars and artisanal on-tap offerings reflecting a change in the city's drinking habits.

The increasing number of innovative brewers who have decided to call Paris and its surrounding suburbs home are the driving force behind this microbrew movement.

Scottish-born and France-based brewer Craig Allen is often cited as an inspiration to Parisian brewers. Allen's hoppy and subtly bitter beers challenged the standard Stella Artois and Kronenberg-style industrial beers that the Parisian palette had become accustomed to. Allen's microbrews have provided an example of what French-based brewers are capable of and have encouraged a new generation of craft brewers in the country. Mixing brewing styles of great beer nations—the UK, Belgium, and the United States—this new generation of brewers is changing the way the French drink beer.

It is impossible to talk about the Paris beer movement without giving credit to Simon Thillou, owner of craft beer boutique La Cave à Bulles (45 rue Quincampoix, 4th arrondissement). The first to feature many local brews as well as great imports from abroad, Simon's cave is a destination for beer lovers in Paris, and Simon himself is an encyclopedia of knowledge when it comes to the French beer scene. Committed to stocking a percentage of his shop with French beers, Simon's job is getting much easier with the increasing number of breweries opening up in and around Paris.

The new wave of Paris-based breweries largely began with Thierry Roche, who opened the Brasserie de la Goutte d'Or in 2012. Inspired by the spices, smells, and street names of the animated Goutte d'Or neighborhood and its African market, Thierry makes beers that reflect local flavor and a sense of

Thierry Roche of Brasserie de la Goutte d'Or.

place. Named after the rues of his corner of the 18th arrondissement, his beers have seen widespread success, with Ernestine—the brewery's IPA, with hints of rooibos and kola nut—frequently selling out at beer bars and boutiques across the capital.

In 2013 Thierry was joined by three other Île-de-France brewers when craft beer was featured for the first time at Montmartre's annual *Fête des Vendanges* (page 2). Completing the quartet of local brewers were Outland, Volcelest, and My Beer Company. The team set the mood for a collaborative and supportive approach to beer-making in Paris and its surrounding suburbs. This sense of community is something that Thomas Deck appreciated when he and his brewing partner, Mike Donohue, opened their Montreuil-based brewery Deck & Donohue in 2014. Thomas points out that he appreciated "the camaraderie that exists within the brewing community." He explains

Claudia and Francois of Le Supercoin.

that "even in its infancy, the greater Parisian group of brewers seems to be ready to stick together and help each other out."

Crucial to the continuation of the beer boom in Paris are the bars and shops that stock local brews. A neighborhood favorite and quintessential hole-in-the-wall bar, Le Supercoin (3 rue Baudelique, 18th arrondissement) stands out by featuring only French artisanal beers handpicked by Claudia, the knowledgeable owner. The bar also has a rotating selection of local beers on tap and an impressive choice of *bières françaises* by the bottle. L'Express de Lyon (1 rue de Lyon, 12th arrondissement) is located in a former PMU—a bar where bets can be made on horse races—and sets a no-frills atmosphere for drinking exciting craft brews from both the old and new worlds. The rotating on-tap menu features a varied selection of IPAs, blondes, *bières blanche*, and stouts. Les Trois 8 (11 rue Victor Letalle, 20th arrondissement) offers both microbrews and natural wines, bringing beer lovers and oenophiles together over one of the best cheese and charcuterie plates in the city. La Fine Mousse

(6 avenue Jean Aicard, 11th arrondissement) boasts over a dozen beers on tap with 150 bottles of artisanal brews on the menu.

Since Simon and La Cave à Bulles paved the way, many other beer shops have followed suit, with La Moustache Blanche (16 rue des Tournelles, 4th arrondissement), People's Drugstore (78 rue des Martyrs, 18th arrondissement), Bières Cultes (locations in the 1st, 5th, 17th, and 18th arrondissements), A La Bière Comme A La Bière (20 rue Custine, 18th arrondissement), which also has a second location (33 rue des Pyrennées, 20th arrondissement) that offers growlers of beer to enjoy on site or take home, and Biérocratie (32 rue de l'Espérance, 13th arrondissement) are among many other boutiques featuring Île-de-France brewed beers.

SUMMER RECIPES

APPETIZERS, SIDES, SALADS, AND SOUPS

FIVE HERB BAKED TOMATOES / *TOMATES PROVENÇALES*

The arrival of summer tomatoes is such an exciting event that early dishes of the season tend to leave them untouched, preserving their wonderful raw flavor. This simple baked tomato recipe celebrates the essence of this seasonal favorite while complementing the flavor with the addition of Herbes de Provence.

Ingredients

Serves 4
8 medium-sized round tomatoes
¼ cup (60 mL) + 1 tablespoon extra virgin olive oil
2 tablespoons Herbes de Provence (oregano, marjoram, rosemary, thyme—avoid the mixture that includes lavender)
4 cloves garlic, chopped
1 pinch of sea salt
Fresh parsley or basil, coarsely chopped

Preparation

Preheat oven to 400°F (200°C). Cut tomatoes, about ½ inch (2 cm) from top, and arrange, cut side up. Lightly coat a baking dish with 1 tablespoon of olive oil. Arrange tomatoes in dish so that they fit snugly together. Sprinkle each tomato with Herbes de Provence and chopped garlic. Drizzle ¼ cup of olive oil over tomatoes. Place in oven on the top rack and bake for 20–30 minutes, or until garlic becomes golden and tomatoes have begun to give their juices while still maintaining their form. Serve warm, topped with a pinch of sea salt and fresh basil or parsley.

FAISSELLE CHEESE WITH FRESH CHIVES AND TOAST / TARTINE DE FAISELLE DE CHÈVRE

This recipe comes from the talented musician and cherished vendanges partner Benjamin Nerot (page 12), who made this recipe as an apèro before we gathered for family dinners during harvest season in the Loire. Faisselle cheese is a creamy raw cheese with no rind. Named after the faisselle, a type of basket that was used to drain the cheese, this particular cheese is often made with goat's milk and is popular in chèvre-producing regions in France. While faisselle cheese resembles yogurt, it lends itself more to savory pairings. Mixed with fresh chives and ground black pepper, it makes a simple appetizer to spread on toasted baguette slices.

Ingredients

Serves 6

1½ cups (400 grams) faisselle, or creamy, goat's cheese

3 tablespoons fresh chives, chopped

Juice from ½ lemon

Freshly ground black pepper

1–2 tablespoons extra virgin olive oil

1 baguette, cut into ½-inch (2 cm) slices and toasted

Preparation

Place cheese in a medium bowl. Stir in 2 tablespoons of the chives, lemon juice, and freshly ground pepper. Season with a thin stream of olive oil to taste. Cover and store in refrigerator. Remove cheese mixture from refrigerator at least 15 minutes before serving. Before serving, toast baguette slices until crisp and golden. Prepare tartines by spreading cheese mixture on toast. Top with remaining chives and serve immediately.

BAVARIAN PRETZELS / *BRETZELS BAVAROIS*

This recipe comes from a Bavarian friend of Café Lomi chef Mardi Hartzog (page 87). Mardi and her business partner, Nichole Richardson, introduced these pretzels to Paris for one of their Parasites events when they took over a local craft beer bar. The pretzels go great with beer, especially lagers. Served with a mustard or butter dipping sauce, they make the perfect snack to go with a locally brewed beer!

Ingredients

Makes 10 pretzels

2 cups (480 mL) skim milk
⅓ cup (40 grams) dry yeast
5 cups (600 grams) all purpose flour
2 teaspoons salt
1 cup (240 mL) water
4 tablespoons baking soda

Toppings:
Large grain salt
Sesame seeds

Preparation

Preheat oven to 375°F (190°C). Heat milk in a small or medium saucepan until lukewarm.

Transfer to a bowl and add dry yeast. Add flour and salt and mix together well, using a fork to scrape together, and then finishing by folding together with your hands. Once the dough is combined, cover with a damp cloth and let sit in a warm place to rise for about 30 minutes. After the dough has risen, separate into 10 equal parts and roll into balls on a floured surface. Once finished, roll each ball into a long strip that is thicker in its center. When you fold your pretzel, make sure to secure the "feet" of the pretzel by pushing them firmly on either side of the bigger section. While you are rolling out your pretzels, combine water and baking soda into a medium pot and bring to a boil. When you have finished folding your dough into a pretzel shape, drop them one at a time into the water and baking soda solution, letting them soak for about 30 seconds and removing with a slotted spoon and setting them directly on a baking sheet lined with parchment paper. Add your toppings of choice, or make a variation of plain, salted, and with sesame seeds. Bake for 15 minutes, or until dark brown.

SPICY HONEY MUSTARD DIPPING SAUCE

Ingredients

3 tablespoons Dijon mustard
2 tablespoons honey
Fresh parsley or chives, finely
    chopped

Preparation

Mix together mustard and honey until fully combined. Top with chopped chives or parsley before serving.

CHIVE BUTTER

Ingredients

½ cup (100 grams) salted butter,
    softened
1 tablespoon chives, finely
    chopped

Preparation

With a whisk, whip together chives and butter until fully combined. Right before serving, heat the butter mixture in a small saucepan over medium-low heat. Let butter simmer for about 5 minutes and serve immediately.

CITRUS DRESSED CARROT SALAD /
SALADE DES CAROTTES RÂPÉES

This ubiquitous salad turns up everywhere in France, from school cafeterias to family dinners. At its base, the recipe is simply lightly dressed carrots, but additions are allowed to be paired with finely grated carrots. Fresh squeezed lemon juice makes for a refreshing dressing when mixed with olive oil. A *Dijon Vinaigrette* (page 150) also works with this salad. Some use white onions, or omit them all together. I use chopped shallots in place of onions—a special touch one of my favorite French grandmothers taught me.

Ingredients

6 large carrots, peeled and grated
3 medium shallots, chopped
4 tablespoons extra virgin olive
    oil
3 teaspoons fresh squeezed
    lemon juice
Salt and pepper

Preparation

In a large salad bowl, toss together grated carrots with chopped shallots. In a small bowl, whisk together olive oil and lemon juice. Dress salad, adding a dash of salt and pepper and tossing until carrots are covered with dressing.

SAUCE

SAUCE PROVENÇAL

This recipe is an elaboration on the Sauce Tomat, one of France's five mother sauces, a list that includes *Béchamel* (page 99), Velouté, Espagnole, and *Hollandaise* (page 38). Giving a classic tomato sauce a southern kick, Sauce Provençal brings together summer ingredients and cooks them down slowly, making a delicious sauce to serve immediately with pasta,

polenta, chicken, or fresh fish, for example. You can conserve this sauce, either by freezing or canning it, for a spot of sunshine during the colder seasons.

Ingredients

Serves 4

2 tablespoons olive oil

4 garlic cloves, minced or pressed

2 cups (300 grams) chopped onions

10 large ripe tomatoes, peeled and coarsely chopped

4 bell peppers, coarsely chopped

2 medium eggplants, coarsely chopped

4 zucchini, coarsely chopped

¼ teaspoon thyme

¼ teaspoon fennel seeds

2 cups (480 mL) dry white wine

Salt and pepper

Chopped fresh parsley (optional)

Preparation

Heat olive oil in a large saucepan, then sauté garlic and onions over medium heat until onions begin to lightly sweat, 5–7 minutes. Add tomatoes. Cook until they begin to soften and give their juice, 8–10 minutes. Add bell peppers, eggplant, zucchini. Stir in thyme and fennel seeds. Add dry white wine. Cover and cook until the vegetables are tender, 15–20 minutes for a thicker, chunkier sauce and 30–45 minutes for a thinner sauce. If you want the sauce to be liquid, you can use an immersion blender to mix the sauce once you've removed it from heat. Season with salt and pepper to taste. If serving immediately, garnish with fresh chopped parsley.

MAINS

END-OF-SUMMER PISTOU SOUP / *SOUPE AU PISTOU*

This is one of my favorite end-of-summer recipes, when the markets are bursting with the best of the summer months while welcoming the vegetables that announce the arrival of autumn. Leeks, onions, and potatoes pair up with summer squash, basil, and ripe tomatoes to create an ideal soup to enjoy at the end of the ever-shorter last days of summer. The beauty of this soup is there is no broth to prepare; the veggies create their own as you go. Feel free to add any other veggies—such as carrots or celery—for flavor.

Ingredients

For the soup:
1½ cups (300 grams) beans (dried or fresh) of your choice (navy or kidney beans work well)
2 tablespoons extra virgin olive oil
1 medium yellow onion, chopped
1 leek, cut into ½ slices
2 large yellow potatoes, cubed
2 teaspoons thyme
1 dried bay leaf
1 zucchini, cut into ½ slices
1 cup (200 grams) green beans, ends removed and cut in half
3 large tomatoes, chopped
1½ cups (250 grams) elbow pasta
Salt and pepper

Preparation

If using dried beans, soak overnight and then cook in boiling water for 1 hour before using. In a large pot, heat olive oil on medium-high heat. Add onion and leek and cook until onion is translucent, 3–5 minutes. Add potatoes, thyme, bay leaf, and a dash of salt and pepper and cook another 5 minutes, stirring occasionally to keep ingredients from sticking to the pot. Add zucchini and green beans and cook 5 minutes. Add tomatoes and beans, then cover and cook on medium heat for 10 minutes. Uncover and add enough water to submerge the veggies. Stir in pasta and bring to a boil. Cook for another 10–15 minutes, or until pasta is done. Season with salt and pepper to taste.

While waiting for pasta to cook, prepare the pistou. Using a mortar and pestle (or a food processor), mash together garlic with a pinch of sea salt. Add chopped basil leaves, pounding or pulsing until

For the pistou:

1 clove garlic

1 pinch sea salt

2 cups (1 bunch) fresh basil
  leaves, chopped

¼ cup (60 mL) extra virgin olive
  oil

4 tablespoons finely grated
  Parmesan cheese

mixture becomes a rough paste, smooth but not liquid. Slowly add olive oil while pounding/pulsing until combined. Stir in cheese and season with salt to taste. Serve soup immediately, topped with a spoonful of pistou and sprinkled with Parmesan cheese.

NIÇOISE SALAD / *SALADE NIÇOISE*

There is much debate about how to make a "vrai," or true, Salade Niçoise. Natives of Nice maintain that their city's salad should only be made using raw ingredients, aside from the hard-boiled eggs and grilled tuna. Purists go as far as to argue that the salad should be composed of simply tomatoes, anchovies, and olives. In Paris you will see many variations, with copious amounts of *crudités* and often the scandalous addition of lettuce—a definite Salade Niçoise no-no. Paris markets are full of perfect farm-fresh veggies in spring and summer that lend themselves to this classic salad. This recipe is for purists, but if you want to break with tradition feel free to add other seasonal vegetables such as radish, violet artichokes, or red onions.

Ingredients

Makes 1 salad
1 clove garlic
Extra virgin olive oil
Salt and pepper
1 medium tomato, quartered
½ cucumber, thinly sliced
½ red bell pepper, julienned
1 green onion, chopped
6–12 black olives
1 medium hard-boiled egg, cut into ½ slices
¼ pound (100 grams) grilled tuna or 4 fillets of marinated anchovies
3–5 small fresh basil leaves

Preparation

Cut clove of garlic in half and use to rub the insides of your salad bowl. Cover the bottom of the salad bowl with olive oil and a dash of salt and pepper. Toss together tomato, cucumber, bell pepper, green onion, and olives. Serve on individual plates, topping with sliced hard-boiled egg and grilled tuna or marinated anchovies. Sprinkle with fresh basil leaves and serve immediately.

FRESH FISH STEW / *BOUILLABAISSE*

This recipe comes from my friend Emma Bentley, who runs a series of Burnt Food supper clubs in the 18th arrondissement. An extension of her blog, *Burnt Cream*, the Burnt Food (and their boozy Burnt Wine counterparts) are a great way to meet people in Paris while enjoying a home-cooked meal and discovering exciting wines and creative cocktails. Emma shared her technique for making this classic French dish, which we later enjoyed on her amazing sun-soaked balcony.

Ingredients

Serves 4

1 pound (450 grams) large raw shrimp, with shells
3 pounds (1½ kilos) of fresh white meat fish fillets
1 pound (450 grams) mussels, with shells
1 tablespoon extra virgin olive oil
1 yellow onion, diced
2 cloves garlic, diced
2 cups (480 mL) water
2–3 yellow potatoes, cut into large cubes
2 large tomatoes, chopped
½ cup (120 mL) dry white wine
1 bay leaf
1 teaspoon thyme
Salt and pepper
1–2 tablespoons fresh dill

Preparation

Thoroughly wash fish and shellfish, scrubbing the mussel shells and removing beards. Remove shrimp shells, setting shells and heads aside in a separate bowl. Heat olive oil in a large pot and add sea salt and shrimp shells and heads. Cook until shells have turned pink, stirring frequently to avoid sticking to the pot. Remove shells and heads and add onion. Cook onion for 2–3 minutes then add garlic. Add water and simmer for 5 minutes. Add potatoes, tomatoes, white wine, bay leaf, thyme, and a dash of salt and pepper; bring to a boil. Cook until potatoes begin to soften, about 15–20 minutes. Add shrimp and white fish and cook another 5 minutes, then add mussels and cook an additional 5 minutes, or until the mussels have all opened their shells. Adjust seasoning to taste and serve immediately, garnished with fresh dill and croutons with a *Rouille* sauce (page 32).

CROUTONS

A great way to use up a baguette before it goes bad, and indispensable for accompaniments to *Fish Soup* (page 30) or *French Onion Soup* (page 97), these croutons can be easily made while preparing your meal—just keep an eye on them at the end, as they can go from golden to charred in the blink of an eye!

Ingredients

1 baguette, cut into about ¼-inch
   (1 cm) slices
2–3 tablespoons extra virgin
   olive oil

Preparation

Preheat oven to 400°F (200°C). Spread baguette slices in one layer on a baking dish. Brush each slice lightly with olive oil, evenly coating each slice. Place baking dish on the middle rack in the oven and bake for 8–10 minutes, checking frequently after they've been in the oven for 5 minutes to avoid burning.

STEWED SUMMER VEGETABLES WITH POACHED EGG / RATATOUILLE AUX OEUFS POCHÉS

A summer classic, this fuss-free dish brings together the all-star vegetables of the season and lets them stew in their own juices until they reach melt-in-your-mouth perfection. Topped with a poached egg and paired with a side of rustic bread to sop up the juices, this makes a perfect midday meal. Enjoy with a chilled glass of rosé!

Ingredients

Serves 4

2 tablespoons olive oil

1 medium onion, diced

2 cloves garlic, chopped

1½ teaspoons thyme

1 sprig fresh or 1 teaspoon dried rosemary

1 large red bell pepper, coarsely chopped

3 zucchini, cut into ½ inch slices

1 large eggplant, cubed

5 large tomatoes, coarsely chopped

Salt and pepper to taste

4 poached eggs

6–8 large fresh basil leaves

Preparation

Heat olive oil in a large pot. Add onion, garlic, thyme, rosemary, and a generous dash of salt and pepper and cook until onions are translucent (8–10 minutes). Add bell pepper, zucchini, and eggplant to pot and cook, stirring occasionally, for 10 minutes. Stir in tomatoes and cover. Let cook 20–25 minutes, or until vegetables are soft and tomatoes have broken down and given their juice. Season with salt and pepper to taste. Serve topped with a poached egg and sprinkled with fresh basil leaves.

TANGY TOMATO MUSTARD TART /
TARTE TOMATE À LA MOUTARDE

This tart is great for a light lunch accompanied with a green salad. You can dress it up by adding basil or mozzarella, but I like to keep it simple, using just a touch of Parmesan and letting the flavor of vine-ripe tomatoes stand out. The tang of Dijon mustard creates a nice balance with the sweetness of the tomatoes and the light seasoning of Herbes de Provence.

Ingredients

Serves 4
Pâte Brisée (page 48)
2–3 tablespoons of Dijon
    mustard
4–5 large ripe tomatoes
1 tablespoon olive oil
2 teaspoon Herbes de Provence
1 pinch sea salt
1 tablespoon grated Parmesan

Preparation

Preheat oven to 375°F (190°C). Roll out pâte brisée and use to line a buttered 10–12 inch tart pan. Poke the bottom with a fork. Spread a thin layer of Dijon mustard on the bottom of the crust. Arrange ¼-inch slices of tomato in the pan in a circular pattern, with slight overlap. Drizzle olive oil over tomatoes then sprinkle with herbes de provence, a pinch of sea salt, and Parmesan. Bake for 25–30 minutes or until tomatoes are golden brown.

DESSERTS

COUNTRYSIDE CHERRY CLAFOUTIS / *CLAFOUTIS AUX CERISES*

This classic French dessert is a summertime favorite. Usually made with cherries or grapes once the end-of-summer harvest season arrives, you can modify the recipe to use whichever fruit you choose, such as black currant, peaches, or raspberries.

Ingredients

Serves 6

¼ cup (60 grams) butter + 1 tablespoon

2 eggs + 2 egg yolks

5 tablespoons (60 grams) sugar

1 teaspoon vanilla extract

5 tablespoons (40 grams) flour

1 cup (240 mL) milk

4 cups (560 grams) ripe, pitted cherries

Preparation

Preheat oven to 375°F (200°C). Use 1 tablespoon of butter to coat a 12-inch pie tin. In a large mixing bowl, beat eggs and egg yolks until combined. Stir in sugar and vanilla extract. Slowly add flour, stirring until combined. Melt ¼ cup butter and add to the egg mixture. Stir in milk. Stir in cherries. Pour mixture into buttered pie tin. Bake for 40–45 minutes, or until golden on top. Serve warm.

FRENCH TOAST WITH BERRY SYRUP / PAIN PERDU AVEC SIROP DES FRUITS ROUGES

Pain perdu, or "lost bread," is the brilliant French solution to using leftover bread. This easy breakfast can be made using any leftover bread, but I always use a baguette, the official bread of Paris, when I make pain perdu. Just make sure that whatever bread you use has hardened enough to soak up the egg mixture while holding its form during cooking. You can top with powdered or unrefined sugar, but during the summer months a simple berry syrup makes a lovely accompaniment to French toast.

Ingredients

Makes about a dozen slices
1 cup (240 mL) milk
3 medium-sized eggs
½ cup (100 grams) sugar
1 day-old baguette, cut into equal size slices (about 1 inch / 2½ cm thick)
1 tablespoon (15 grams) butter

Preparation

In a medium bowl, whisk together milk, eggs, and sugar. Dunk baguette slices in the egg mixture, coating evenly. Melt butter on medium heat in a pan. Place batter-soaked bread slices in the pan and cook on each side, about 1–2 minutes each, until golden. Serve immediately topped with powdered or unrefined sugar or berry syrup.

For the syrup:
Seasonal berries are perfect for this simple syrup. This mixed berry syrup is a nice fruity topping for French toast. *Black Currant Syrup* (page 171) also pairs well with this breakfast dish.

Ingredients

Makes about 2 cups (480 mL)
2 cups (400 grams) sugar
4 cups (960 mL) water
2 cups (250 grams) mixed
berries, such as strawberries
(halved), raspberries, or
blueberries

Preparation

In a saucepan, stir sugar in water to dissolve, then bring to a boil. Add berries and bring water to a boil again. Reduce heat to medium and cook for 15–20 minutes, using a wooden spoon occasionally to crush the berries, getting them to release their juice. Remove from heat. Keep the syrup chunky by straining off only a little liquid and keeping the remaining strawberry pieces or, for a thinner syrup, strain entire mixture into a glass jar and keep only the juice for your syrup. Let cool and then refrigerate for up to one week.

LEMON ZEST MADELEINES / *MADELEINES*

As *Gateaux Mama* founder Melanie Vaz will attest, the true challenge in making a Madeleine is "getting the bump." This talented local baker kindly guided me in the quest to make the perfect madeleine. A combination of patience while chilling the dough and kicking the temperature up a notch for the last few minutes led us to this recipe, which delivers golden, lemony madeleines, complete with their signature humped back. For a floral touch, add dried lavender to your batter before baking.

You'll need nonstick madeleine molds for this recipe, which you can find in most Paris cookware shops (page 60) or a well-equipped cooking store near you. A piping bag is helpful when filling the molds, but not obligatory.

Ingredients

Makes about a dozen madeleines

¾ stick (75 grams) butter + 1 tablespoon

¾ cup (85 grams) sifted flour

¾ tablespoon double acting baking powder

Pinch of salt

½ cup (100 grams) sugar

Zest of 1 lemon

Juice of 1 lemon

2 medium eggs

1 teaspoon dried lavender (optional)

Preparation

Chill madeleine molds in refrigerator for at least 30 minutes. Preheat oven to 400°F (210°C). Melt butter and let cool. Remove chilled madeleine molds and use the tablespoon of melted butter to brush, coating evenly. Dust with flour and tap to remove excess, leaving a thin layer. Return madeleine molds to refrigerator. Whisk together flour, baking powder, and salt. Using a hand mixer, combine sugar, lemon zest and lemon juice. Beat in eggs one by one and continue to mix for another 2–3 minutes, until batter is a pale yellow. Fold in dry ingredients (including lavender, if using), followed by the rest of the melted butter. Transfer batter to a piping bag, if using; otherwise, cover in a bowl and let chill in the refrigerator for at least 1 hour. Pipe (or spoon) batter into each individual mold, filling up only about ⅔ of the way. Lightly tap the mold to evenly distribute batter and remove air bubbles. Place in the refrigerator to chill for another 30–60 minutes. Bake in oven for 11–13 minutes, until golden brown. Remove immediately from molds by gently tapping until they fall out. Let cool on a cooling rack until warm or at room temperature.

ACKNOWLEDGMENTS

This book is as much a guide to Paris as it is a thank you to the city and its people. Moving to Paris changed my life in ways I never thought possible, and I cherish those who have shared the adventure with me. Living abroad has not always been easy, mostly for my parents David and Sandra. Thanks, mom and dad, for sharing your daughter with Paris and always encouraging me to find my happiness, whether at home or abroad. Thanks to my sisters, Cézanne and Audrey, for being my best forever friends and making life more fun. Thanks to Grandpa Jack for your excitement and stories, and thanks to Simone Barrot for the inspiration for so many of the recipes in this book.

I am grateful to the Paris Ladies Collective for their constant support and encouragement, particularly Melanie Vaz for the intensive baking lessons and recipe testing sessions, Forest Collins for her collaborations and pep talks, and Kim Laidlaw, for being a unicorn. Thanks to my urban family for all the dinner/dance parties that provided the opportunity to test recipes (and my neighbors' patience). Pirate Luc Revel, thank you for the bubbles and brunches. Thanks to the crew at Holybelly for being the unofficial headquarters of an intimate book club made up of me and some of my favorite ladies. Jessie Kanelos Weiner, Kristen Beddard, and Anna Brones, you inspire me every day, I'm so grateful I met you, and I'm lucky to call you friends.

To my agent, Deborah Ritchken, and my editor, Joseph Sverchek, thank you for believing in this project and making it a reality. Thank you also to Amanda Matteo at Skyhorse for the many hours you put into this book. My eternal gratitude goes to Nicholas Ball for all the gorgeous photo shoots, darling.

I am thankful for so many people I met during the process of writing this book. Noella Morantin, thank you for letting me join your team; 2014 was a *grand cru*. Laurent Saillard, for everything you've taught me, in and out of the vines. Ben Nerot, I met you in the middle of this book, but can't imagine it existing without you—thank you for all the late night recipe (and wine) tastings, the constant encouragement, and for reminding me of what's important in life.

Finally, thank you to all the independent farmers, chefs, bakers, baristas, bartenders, brewers, and small business owners who make up the changing landscape of this city and make it so fun for the rest of us to explore—this book is ultimately for, and about, you.

RECIPE AND INGREDIENT INDEX

SUBJECT AND NAME INDEX